Budgets and Financial Management in Higher Education

Budgets and Financial Management in Higher Education

Margaret J. Barr,
George S. McClellan

JOSSEY-BASS
A Wiley Imprint
www.josseybass.com

Published by Jossey-Bass
A Wiley Imprint
989 Market Street, San Francisco, CA 94103-1741—www.josseybass.com

Jossey-Bass books and products are available through most bookstores. To contact Jossey-Bass directly call our Customer Care Department within the U.S. at 800-956-7739, outside the U.S. at 317-572-3986, or fax 317-572-4002.

Jossey-Bass also publishes its books in a variety of electronic formats. Some content that appears in print may not be available in electronic books.

Library of Congress Cataloging-in-Publication Data

Barr, Margaret J.
　　Budgets and financial management in higher education / Margaret J. Barr, George S. McClellan.
　　　　p. cm. — (The Jossey-Bass higher and adult education series)
　　Includes bibliographical references and index.
　　ISBN 978-0-470-61620-8 (hardback); ISBN 978-0-470-92312-2 (ebk);
　　ISBN 978-0-470-92313-9 (ebk); ISBN 978-0-470-92315-3 (ebk)
　　　　1. Education, Higher—United States—Finance.　2. Universities and colleges—United States—Business management.　I. McClellan, George S.　II. Title.
　　LB2342.B3245　2011
　　378.1'06—dc22

2010037992

Printed in the United States of America
FIRST EDITION
HB Printing　10 9 8 7 6 5 4 3 2

The Jossey-Bass
Higher and Adult Education Series

Contents

Figures, Tables, and Exhibits

Exhibits

Preface

Most administrators in institutions of higher education carry responsibility for budget management. It may be only one of many parts of their responsibilities but it is critical to their success. Individuals charged with budget responsibility, however, often do not have training or experience in managing this important function. Assumptions are often made that because a person is experienced in program development, teaching, or research that they are familiar with the basic principles of budgeting and financial management. This is not necessarily true, and this volume has been written to fill part of that gap in knowledge and experience.

The target audiences for the volume include managers in a variety of roles within higher education, including director, dean, vice president, department chair, coordinator, and program director. Graduate students studying higher education administration at both the master's and doctoral level will also find this version of the book to be useful. This volume is intended for those with limited exposure to higher education budgets and fiscal management. Written in plain language, it is intended for readers who do not have a strong background in matters financial.

This text is based on a successful 2002 monograph, *The Jossey-Bass Academic Administrator's Guide to Budgets and Financial Management*. The original monograph was focused on helping those new to budget responsibilities in academic affairs understand the language and the processes of budget management in higher education. This edition builds on that work but expands it in some critical areas, including an expanded focus on budget models in higher education and an expanded discussion of the fiscal management of auxiliary enterprises. The text has also been expanded to address the broader audience of those with new or expanded budget responsibilities in higher education and to include a more in-depth discussion of the factors involved in developing and implementing an institutional budget. Information has been updated throughout the text to reflect contemporary conditions in higher education. Auxiliary and capital budgets are covered in greater depth in a separate chapter. A case study involving budget increases at Alpha University in Chapter One provides an opportunity for readers to apply information learned to an actual situation. The fictional Alpha University is referenced many times in subsequent chapters to illustrate important concepts. Alpha University is revisited in another case study in Chapter Seven and provides an opportunity for readers to apply what they have learned. Chapter Seven also contains a case study on Omega College added to illustrate the unique challenges facing smaller, private, tuition-dependent universities. Each chapter closes with a set of reflective questions to help the reader apply the information to the specific set of circumstances and challenges that they face.

Chapter One, "The Fiscal Context and the Role of the Budget Manager," discusses the broader fiscal forces that influence funding in American higher education. In addition, the chapter contains a discussion of the role of a budget manager (whether it is a full or part-time responsibility) within a budgetary unit and within the greater institutional environment. Chapter Two, "Primary Elements of the Budget: Revenue and Expenses," presents the various sources of revenue and the broad categories of expenses that characterize budgets in higher education. Attention is given to the issues that should be confronted when dealing with revenue and expenses. Chapter Three, "Understanding Budgets," discusses the purposes of the budget, the different types of budgets, and the different budget models that may be part of the responsibility of any administrator in higher education. In Chapter Four, "Management of the Budget Cycle," the discussion centers on the ongoing nature of budget management and the need to understand the past, present, and future fiscal issues of the budget unit. Auxiliary enterprises and capital budgets provide special issues in fiscal management. Chapter Five, "Understanding Auxiliary and Capital Budgets," clarifies the challenges and opportunities facing budget managers dealing with those enterprises. Any administrative position is fraught with problems that must be solved and pitfalls that should be avoided; budget management is no exception. Chapter Six, "Problems and Pitfalls in Budget Management," discusses those issues in detail and suggests how to confront problems and avoid pitfalls. Finally, Chapter Seven, "Managing Budget Fluctuations," offers suggestions on how to manage both budget cuts and new resources flowing into the institution and budget unit. Also in Chapter Seven, Alpha University is revisited in an additional case study with budget reductions as the task for the reader. Chapter Seven also contains a new case study on Omega college that permits the reader to apply the information learned throughout the volume. The book concludes with a Glossary of Terms, which we hope will be helpful to readers in understanding the terminology used throughout the volume as well as in their daily work as budget managers within an institution of higher education.

Acknowledgments

Peggy Barr would like to thank her colleagues at several institutions for helping her gain an understanding of financial matters in higher education. Those individuals include John Pembroke, Leigh Secrest, the late Bill Fischer, Gene Sunshine, Sheila Driscoll, and Eric Wachtel. She would also like to thank her family and friends for their support and her colleague George McClellan for his quality contributions to the volume.

George McClellan is grateful to all those who have helped shape his journey in the student affairs profession, not the least of whom are the students who have allowed him in ways direct and indirect to be a part of their amazing stories. Particular thanks go to two colleagues at Indiana University–Purdue University Fort Wayne: Chancellor Mike Wartell for his continued support for George's efforts as a practitioner scholar and Dave Reynolds for being a truly wonderful budget manager. Last but not least, George is particularly thankful to Peggy Barr for being his mentor, friend, and partner for this project.

Our purpose was to write a book that instructs, informs, and aids our colleagues who are facing fiscal management responsibilities as part of their responsibilities. We hope it does that.

Margaret J. Barr
Evanston, Illinois
George S. McClellan
Fort Wayne, Indiana

About the Authors

Margaret J. Barr served as vice president for student affairs at Northwestern University from October 1992 until July 2000 when she retired. She currently is professor emeritus in the School of Education and Social Policy at Northwestern and is engaged in part-time consulting, writing, and volunteer work. Prior to her appointment at Northwestern, she was vice chancellor for student affairs at Texas Christian University for eight years. She also served as vice president for student affairs at Northern Illinois University from 1982 to 1985 and was assistant vice president for student affairs at that same institution from 1980 to 1982. She was first assistant and then associate dean of students at the University of Texas at Austin from 1971 through 1980. She has also served as director of housing and director of the college union at Trenton State College and assistant director and director of women's residences at the State University of New York at Binghamton.

In her various administrative roles, Barr has always carried responsibilities for supervision of operating budgets. During her eighteen years as a vice president, she supervised operating and reserve budgets for both auxiliary and institutionally allocated budgets. She has been involved in a number of capital projects, including the construction of new residence halls, new recreation facilities, and dining facilities and renovations of multicultural centers, residential units, and an academic advising center.

She has held numerous leadership positions with the American College Personnel Association (ACPA), including a term as president (1983–1984). She has been the recipient of the ACPA Contribution to Knowledge Award (1990) and Professional Service Award (1986) and was an ACPA Senior Scholar from 1986 to 1991.

She also has been active in the National Association of Student Personnel Administrators (NASPA), including service as the director of the NASPA Institute for Chief Student Affairs Officers (1989, 1990) and president of the NASPA Foundation Board (2000–2002). Barr was the recipient of the NASPA Outstanding Contribution to Literature and Research Award in 1986, the award for Outstanding Contribution to Higher Education in 2000, and was named a Pillar of the Profession by the NASPA Foundation in that same year.

She is the author or editor of numerous books and monographs, including, *The Handbook of Student Affairs Administration* (1993), co-editor of the second edition of *The Handbook of Student Affairs Administration* (2000) with M. Desler, co-author of *Critical Issues for Student Affairs* (2006) with Arthur Sandeen, co-editor of *New Futures for Student Affairs* with M. Lee Upcraft (1990), the editor of *Student Affairs and the Law* (1988), and co-editor of *Developing Effective Student Service Programs: A Guide for Practitioners* with L. A. Keating (1985). She served as editor-in-chief for the monograph series *New Directions for Student Services* from 1986 to 1998. She also is the author of numerous books and monograph chapters.

Barr received a bachelor's degree in elementary education from the State University of New York College at Buffalo in 1961 and a master's degree in college student personnel–higher education from Southern Illinois University, Carbondale, in 1964. She received a PhD in educational administration from the University of Texas at Austin in 1980.

George S. McClellan is the vice chancellor for student affairs at Indiana University–Purdue University Fort Wayne (IPFW). Before coming to IPFW, he was vice president for student development at Dickinson State University in Dickinson, North Dakota, and served students in a variety of roles at the University of Arizona and Northwestern University. During his service at Northwestern University, McClellan held a variety of professional positions, which included responsibility for graduate and professional housing, food service, and campus commons. Throughout his career he has had significant responsibility for the development and management of budgets, including auxiliary and capital budgets.

McClellan has served in a variety of leadership positions in student affairs. He is a member of the editorial board of both the *Journal of College Student Development* and the *Journal of College and Character* and was co-editor of the third edition of *The Handbook for Student Affairs Administration* (2009) with Jeremy Stringer. He was a member of the National Association of Student Personnel Administrators (NASPA) Foundation Board and a founding member of that association's Administrators in Graduate and Professional Student Services Community and its Indigenous Peoples Knowledge Community. He served as chair or co-chair of NASPA's Task Force on Gambling and its Ad Hoc Work Group on the Voluntary System of Accountability.

He received the Outstanding Contribution to Research in American Indian Higher Education award from the Native American Network of the American College Personnel Association in 2002. He was recognized by the NASPA Foundation as a Pillar of the Profession in 2010.

McClellan received his PhD in Higher Education from the University of Arizona (2003). Both his M.S.Ed. in Higher Education (1998) and BA in English and American Literature (1982) were earned from Northwestern University.

1

The Fiscal Context and the Role
of the Budget Manager

U nderstanding how to forecast, build, and manage a budget is an essential skill for all administrators in higher education. Almost every administrative position in higher education carries some responsibility for budget management. From a new professional managing a small program budget to a program director to a dean or vice president, understanding the budget and skill in managing budget issues and problems are critical competencies for administrative success.

This chapter focuses on increasing the reader's understanding of the process of obtaining financial support for institutions of higher education. It first addresses the complex fiscal context for American higher education. It then focuses on the differences in fiscal issues between public and private (independent) institutions of higher education. Next it discusses the responsibilities of the person who manages the budget for an individual program, a department, a division, or a school or college within an institution. The chapter closes with a discussion of the importance of this information for any administrator in higher education. At the end of the chapter the practical implications of this information are illustrated in a case study of Alpha University, followed by reflective questions.

The Fiscal Context of American Higher Education

Higher education institutions, whether public or private, are experiencing great changes related to identifying and capturing fiscal resources to support educational endeavors. The broader

1

fiscal context of higher education sets very real constraints on what can and cannot be done in any institution of higher education. These broader fiscal issues include the influence the recession of 2008–2009 has had on the funding for both private and public higher education; increased competition for funds within both the public and private economic sectors; increased regulation, including a rise in unfunded mandates at the state and federal levels; the cost of technology; increased competition for faculty and staff; increased competition for students; concerns about the rising cost of higher education to students and their families; and rising costs for the purchase of goods and services.

The 2008–2009 Recession

Goldstein states: "The economies of all institutions are linked with the national economy which is increasingly connected to the world economy" (2005, p. 14). Never has that statement been clearer than in the years since 2008. The 2008–2009 recession had a profound effect on American higher education in both the public and private sectors. In the public sector, two major issues have been in the news: the reduction of direct state support to the public institutions and the reduction in state grants and scholarships awarded to individual student residents. At least thirty-four states had some reduction in support for public higher education (AASCU, January 2009), with Arizona, California, and Florida being notable examples. In general, state funding for higher education was substantially reduced in FY2009 and further reductions are being anticipated in many public institutions of higher education in the future.

Student applications for financial aid increased as the economy suffered. "The federal government's Pell Grant program, the bellwether of all financial aid programs, has seen a huge increase in the number of applications in light of the economic downturn" (AASCU, 2009, p. 2). The influence of the reductions in direct aid to students at the state level played a significant role in the record growth in enrollments to community college and regional public institutions.

Many states also face reduced tax bases due to high unemployment rates and business closings or reductions and thus could not meet their obligations to state institutions. Illinois and California provide excellent examples of such conditions. Failure of the states to meet their funding obligations to state-supported institutions resulted in actions such as mandatory unpaid furloughs for faculty and staff, reduction in support for equipment replacement, reduction in library support, and postponement of needed repairs and renovations. Some of these measures will have ramifications far into the future for state-supported institutions.

Private higher education has also not been immune from budget cuts. Endowment losses have been quite substantial in some institutions. For example, Harvard University, with the largest higher education endowment in the country, initially lost approximately 27% of their endowment (Zhu, 2009), and they were not alone. Both large and small institutions sustained substantial losses in their endowments, and if the institution was overly dependent on endowment funds for the annual operating budget then budget cuts were inevitable. Even prudent institutions with a spending rule for endowment funds were faced with slowing down growth, forgoing raises, postponing capital projects, and other cost containment measures. Those institutions that relied on an annual fund (donations to the institution during the fiscal year) were also hard pressed to continue all activities, programs, and salary raises if the annual fund drive was not successful. Even prudent institutions had to use a variety of cost-containment measures until the full impact of the economic downturn was determined and economic growth returned.

Increased Competition for Funds

Competition for funds has increased in both the public and private sector over the last decade and is likely to continue into the future. In most states, state government has become a growth industry, with the number and variety of programs funded out of tax support growing each year. Many state health care programs have also expanded to meet the needs of an aging population. Other programs, such as prisons and public safety, have grown because of the increase in criminal behavior and public demand for stricter law enforcement and harsher criminal penalties. The infrastructure of most states, including streets and highways, bridges, tunnels, flood control, and public transportation, are all aging and need massive renovation and repair. Recreational use of public lands has grown and with that growth has come the need to assure the safety and health of members of the public using the lands and additional construction to provide safe access and egress. The list of state needs seems to be never ending. Suffice it to say that higher education is but one of many programs seeking support for a very limited amount of money at the state level (Schuh, 2000). The result has been less and less direct fiscal support for public higher education and increased expectations that such institutions develop new ways to obtain the resources necessary to operate the enterprise. In fact, some public institutions have changed their public rhetoric and describe their institution as state "related" rather than state "supported" because the contribution of the state to the institutional budget has been reduced so much over the last decade of the twentieth century and the first decade of the twenty-first century. The University of Virginia and the University of Vermont are both examples of such institutions.

The reduction in available state funding also influences private higher education in both direct and indirect ways. Directly the institution may not receive funding for a special project that meets the needs of the state (See Chapter Two). Indirectly, state financial aid grants to individual needy students usually can be used by the student at both public and private institutions. If funding for such aid programs is reduced or remains static, more of the cost for individual student aid is shifted to any institution enrolling the student.

During the last decades, many public institutions have also joined their private colleagues in seeking financial support from alumni, foundations, parents, business, and industry. Billion-dollar campaigns, in either the public or private sector of higher education, are no longer unusual and consume a great deal of the time and energy of institutional leaders. Concurrently, other charitable institutions such as museums, youth service organizations, and organizations focusing on diseases and social welfare issues have also increased their quest for financial support. Competition for private funds is fierce and likely to remain so. Consequently, fundraising has become a major function in many institutions.

Increased Regulations and Unfunded Mandates

Within the last fifty years American higher education has experienced unprecedented growth in regulations from both the state and federal governments. Many of these statutory regulations support important opportunities for students, faculty, and staff but they also require additional institutional investment in order to achieve compliance. However, funding for compliance at either the state or federal level has not been forthcoming. Examples of these unfunded mandates include the following:

Security and Safety

The security and safety of students, faculty, and staff has been the subject of a number of federal regulations. For faculty and staff the Occupational Safety and Health Act of 1970 (OSHA) and the Employee Retirement Income Security Act of 1974 (ERISA) both influence the day-by-day working conditions of most faculty and staff members at institutions of higher education. These regulations focus on everything from the disposal of contaminated materials to the configuration of workstations. The Student Right-to-Know and Campus Security Act of 1990 and accompanying Department of Education regulations requires notification of all members of the campus community of crime statistics and other crime data on an annual basis. Depending on how that notification is conducted the costs for printing, mailing, and other means of communication can be quite large.

Student and Employee Privacy

The Family Educational Rights and Privacy Act (FERPA) regulates access to student records and requires institutions to inform students of their rights under the act on an annual basis. Faculty and staff have privacy protections under the National Labor Relations Act of 1935.

Research Regulations

Regulations governing research are many, but two stand out with regard to costs to institutions. The Animal Welfare Act (7 U.S.C. sec. 21.31. *et seq.*) regulates the care of animals used in research on campus. Compliance with the standards required by the federal government under the act has been an expensive investment for most institutions of higher education. Research involving human beings is regulated through the Department of Health and Human Services Policy for Protection of Human Research Subjects (45 CFR 46) and requires disclosure of risks and monitoring of participation of humans involved in research studies. Compliance with research regulations has direct and indirect costs to the institution that are not funded by the granting federal or state agencies, including the hiring of staff to monitor compliance across the institution.

Discrimination

A plethora of laws are in place at the federal level that prohibit discrimination in admission and employment, and all have a real and direct influence on the conduct of daily life in colleges and universities. These laws affect the complexity of searches for positions, record keeping in human resource offices, admissions practices, and intercollegiate athletics. All of these statutes have some monetary costs attached to them. The various discrimination statutes include prohibiting discrimination on the basis of age (Employment Act of 1967) and race, creed, sex, or national origin (Title VII of the Civil Rights Act of 1964, amended by the Equal Employment Opportunity Act of 1972). Title IX prohibits discrimination in educational programs, facilities, policies, and employment practices.

Intercollegiate athletics is the most striking example of rising costs associated with compliance with Title IX. Providing opportunities for young women to receive athletic opportunities in proportion to their enrollment in the institution has been a very positive change, but it is a change that has great costs associated with it, particularly in Division I schools that provide scholarships for both men and women athletes. In addition, Title IX requirements also influence costs associated with team travel and facilities to support athletic endeavors.

The Rehabilitation Act of 1972 prohibits discrimination in access to educational programs for persons with handicaps if they are otherwise qualified. The Americans with Disabilities Act (1990) is targeted toward making programs, facilities, and activities accessible to persons with disabilities. Both statutes are laudable for providing opportunities for higher education to previously underserved populations, but neither of these acts include funding for upgrading facilities to assure compliance.

Achieving compliance can be further complicated by state statutes and local ordinances that prohibit discrimination on the basis of sexual orientation. In addition, many state statutes and local ordinances have more stringent antidiscrimination regulations than those covered in the federal legislation.

Student Financial Aid

Federal student financial aid programs are complex, and the accompanying regulations for Pell Grants, College Work-Study, and various loan programs can be confusing to students and their parents. The burden of helping students and their families understand and access such programs falls on institutions of higher education without any funding at all from either the state or federal level. This might include printing materials in another language, providing online assistance to prospective students and their families, or sending financial aid staff out to areas in which many prospective students reside to provide hands-on assistance to those unfamiliar with applying for financial aid.

Other Issues

There are state statutes involving audit requirements, grant funding and reporting, fiscal management, and fiduciary responsibilities of officers and trustees of institutions of higher education. In addition, there are also federal statutes, which must be complied with for cost sharing in grants and contracts and rules for grants and contracts by the Office of Management and Budget (OMB). None of these requirements come with concomitant funding, which must be borne by the institution.

Cost Concerns

The cost of attendance at institutions of higher education, both public and private, is becoming both a growing societal concern and a political one. Parents, legislators, alumni, and friends of institutions of higher education are all expressing reservations about the rising costs of tuition, fees, and room and board. Boards and commissions at both the federal and state levels have focused on the cost of American higher education (Callan and Finney, 1997; Harvey, 1998; and Lingenfelter, 2004). Wadsworth stated, "Tougher economic times could affect the public's view that anyone who really wants a college education can get one. What's more tougher economic times might well increase families' anxiety about their ability to cover their share of college expenses, as well as the availability of jobs for themselves and their children just coming out of college" (in Immerwahr and Foleno, 2000, p. 34).

The issues related to cost of attendance are also directly linked to financial aid for students. Access and choice have been central to the mission of many public and private institutions. In order to support an economically diverse student body, federal and state governments and institutions of higher education have invested heavily in financial aid to students. As the cost of attendance rises, so do financial aid budgets, and the fiscal resources of all institutions are stretched. The problem is compounded in situations with substantial graduate and professional school academic programs. In such environments, the cost of instruction and research is high and the direct payment by individual students for such educational access is relatively low. The cost of higher education and the funding of financial aid will continue to remain challenges for institutions of higher education.

Cost of Technology

Technology is both a blessing and a curse for institutions of higher education. It is a blessing because it provides new tools for communication, administration, and research. Students and faculty come to any institution with high expectations for technology support, including Internet access, networking, and wireless connectivity, and they want quick and accurate access to information and data. The growth of technology is a curse with respect to cost. In a rapidly evolving technological environment the costs for hardware and software are enormous, and once the initial investment is made costs continue to escalate with every change.

Technology also brings opportunities to change the way any institution of higher education does routine business, from keeping student records to supporting a complex research agenda. The installation and continuous upgrades of student information systems, accounting systems, academic support programs such as Blackboard, financial information systems, purchasing, and human resource management have become very large initial and recurring costs in institutional budgets.

There is also a growing expectation that the communication between the institution and students and potential students, their families, and alumni be strengthened through the use of technology. In addition, students, their families, alumni, prospective employers of students, and donors and friends of the institution all expect easy access to the information they want and need. This does not come without cost for the development and maintenance of Web sites, information portals, e-mail systems, and databases, and the movement of traditional hard copy resources such as a library to digitally accessible systems is both expensive and labor intensive.

In addition, each year new and advanced technological applications are developed to improve instruction and to strengthen communication between instructors and students and between students in a specific class or section. As such new applications are tested and adapted within an academic setting there are increased costs to implement and maintain instructional support.

When the technological revolution in higher education started there was a hope that positions could be eliminated as a result of technology, but that has not proven to be the case. In fact, the growth in the use of technology has brought with it increased competition for qualified technical staff between higher education and business and industry. There are many good reasons for installing technological innovations on a college campus. Saving money is not one of them.

Competition for Faculty and Staff

Higher education has been actively competing with business and industry for both skilled and unskilled workers. The recent economic downturn has eased some of the competition, but for some categories of employees competition with non–higher education positions remains very strong. Technical managers and technical support staff are still in high demand in all sectors of the economy, and the problem of attracting and retaining personnel is not limited to staff ranks. New doctoral candidates and young, talented faculty in business, engineering, and computer sciences continue to be heavily recruited by business and industry.

When economic woes in the nation ease there will again be competition with business and industry for talented faculty and staff in a number of academic disciplines. If turnover is high in some categories of positions then the issue should be carefully studied. Compensation *may* be an issue, but other policies and procedures may also be contributing to the staff turnover problem. When institutions try to attract and retain new faculty and staff, they must assure that those individuals who are currently a part of the work force are not disadvantaged by any strategies used to attract new hires. New approaches to compensation and benefits are being developed at some institutions with the goal of reducing turnover, while at others changes are being made in policies to aid those employed at the institution. Whatever the approach, this issue is likely to have huge financial implications for the institution and every budget unit.

Increased Competition for Students

Competition for students is a constant in higher education. Some institutions are absolutely dependent on enrollment to cover the cost of operations for the fiscal year. The loss of even twenty students (and their tuition dollars) at such institutions can mean the difference between institutional fiscal failure and success. For other institutions, the budget is not as enrollment driven, but policies of providing access and choice to students, referenced earlier, remain at the forefront of fiscal decisions. Competition for students results in higher financial aid budgets and other tuition-discounting schemes, such as a lower tuition rate for a second child from the same family. However, financial aid is often not enough to attract the students desired by the institution. Institutional amenities such as recreation facilities, student centers, wellness centers, residential colleges and the like are becoming more important to prospective students and their parents.

Such amenities do not come without cost, and competition for funds within each institution is likely to increase as the college or university attempts to be more inviting to prospective students.

Finally, the cost of the actual recruitment process continues to grow as each institution attempts to get a specific message out to students and their parents. Technology may help ease some of these costs by using e-mail and social networking sites as new recruitment tools. It is as yet unclear what their effectiveness is in increasing yield and is still being studied.

In addition to recruitment efforts for traditionally aged students, many institutions have sought new markets for their educational programs by embracing adult and returning students. Creation of education and support programs for nontraditional students is not an inexpensive undertaking. With new markets come new demands for services. It is a volatile, changing, and risky environment, and the costs associated with recruitment and retention of students must be considered in the development of each annual institutional budget.

Rising Costs of Goods and Services

The Consumer Price Index (CPI) is the standard used to measure the growth or decline of the cost of goods and services in the general economy. The Higher Education Price Index (HEPI) differs from the CPI in that it focuses on a range of goods and services that are usually purchased by institutions of higher education and it also includes faculty and staff salaries, purchased services such as telecommunications, and commodities such as books, periodicals, supplies, equipment, and utilities (Goldstein, 2005). A more focused index has been developed by the State Higher Education Executive Officers, and use of this index (the Higher Education Cost Adjustment, HECA) demonstrates that the "costs of goods and services in higher education have risen more rapidly than those in the general economy" (Goldstein, 2005, p. 23). Why is this important? Understanding why the costs of goods and services in institutions of higher education have grown so rapidly is an essential first step.

For any institution, exceptional cost increases in any category can cause budget havoc. To illustrate, consider what the unprecedented, nearly 300% increase in the cost of scholarly journals over the past 20 years (Association of Research Libraries, 2005) has done to library budgets. Or consider what a large increase in the cost of water can do to the efficacy of a grounds and maintenance budget or an auxiliary service budget on a residential campus (see Chapter Five on auxiliaries for more information).

Although costs in all sectors of goods and services have risen, only a careful examination of the way business is done in the institution will mitigate rising cost from having an adverse influence on the budget. For example, are there ways to cut energy or water use by the use of innovative technology that can pay for itself within three years? Can the library enter into an alliance with other nearby institutions to share scholarly journals so that all are not purchased by every institution? Are there less expensive ways to communicate with parents and students? Creative solutions are needed for these and other questions.

Differences Between Public and Private Institutions

A number of fund sources support both public and private (independent) institutions of higher education. The emphasis and dependence on each source of financial support will vary between institutions even of the same type. Figure 1.1 graphically illustrates the complexity of funding for both public and private higher education.

Chapter Two reviews the entire range of financial support for both public and private institutions and also focus on the expenses facing higher education entities.

Although in the past the funding for higher education differed markedly between public and private institutions, today those differences are becoming increasingly blurred. Figure 1.2 compares and contrasts the sources of funds for all public and all private not-for-profit institutions of higher education across the

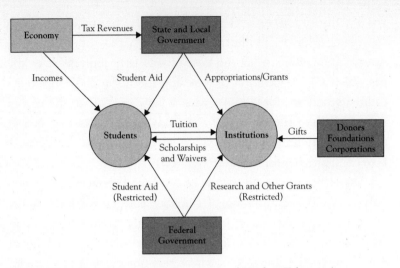

Figure 1.1.   Relationships in Financing of Higher Education
Used with permission of NCHEMS Information Center for Higher Education
Policymaking and Analysis.

country. There are marked differences in the sources of funds in
two areas—state government support and tuition and fees—but
most other areas are comparable between private and public institutions. As demand for the use of state and federal funds for other
purposes continues to grow, public institutions have adopted many
of the strategies of private institutions to obtain funds to support
educational endeavors. The greatest difference between public and
private institutions is the degree of control on matters of finance
that is exercised beyond the campus.

Control and Approvals

In private institutions, financial policies, investment strategies,
and institutional policies are controlled either through the governing board or through other campus-based governance and
administrative bodies. This approach provides greater degrees of
freedom in using resources to meet unexpected needs or problems.
For example, the cost of technology has required reallocation at

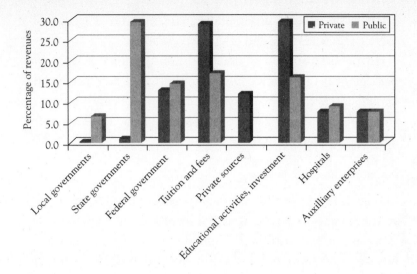

Figure 1.2.   Distribution of Revenues by Source in Higher Education*

Adapted from U.S. Department of Education, National Center for Education Statistics, 2005–06 Integrated Postsecondary Education Data System (IPEDS), 2008, Figures 16 and 17.

*Note that the federal government collects information on revenues from public and private not-for-profit institutions in slightly differing formats. The report for public institutions includes the category "Investment return, gifts, and other" whereas the report for the private institutions includes the category "Educational activities, investment return, and other." The report for private institutions includes the category "Private sources" whereas the report for publics does not.

many private institutions. Permission for that reallocation did not have to be sought beyond the campus. For public institutions often permission must be sought from the system office, the state coordinating board, some other oversight board, or the legislature itself to change the approved uses of legislative appropriations.

Policies

Fiscal policies at private institutions are likely to be less cumbersome because they permit transfers of funds for reasonable purposes without outside approvals and other bureaucratic barriers.

There is great unit accountability, and the unit is examined if there is a deficit at the end of the fiscal year.

In public institutions, usually the institutional budget office must grant permission for line item transfers over a specified dollar amount. Sometimes, for certain categories of expenditures, the governing board or the supervising state higher education agency must approve such transfers.

Human Resource Issues

In both types of institutions, there is concern for unbridled growth in the number of positions at the institution. Adding new positions in public institutions is usually more difficult than in the private sector, although in both arenas the budgeting unit must account for salary or wages and other costs (for example benefits) associated with such positions, and the money must be available to fund the position.

Compensation for faculty and staff are major issues in both public and private institutions. The growth of technology, in particular, has made persons with such backgrounds highly sought after in the marketplace. Higher education, in both sectors, has had to develop new compensation guidelines to keep and attract technical staff, and traditional compensation models do not appear to work at either type of institution.

Unions are present at both public and private institutions and create special human resource issues, including work rules and compensation. A union environment creates proscribed conditions for handling issues of employee discipline, workloads, benefits, and financial reward structures.

Both types of institutions also must comply with state and federal regulations and laws relating to issues of equal opportunity, disabilities, sexual harassment, worker's compensation, civil rights, and health and safety. The budget is also intertwined with a number of legal and institutional requirements regarding personnel. To illustrate, there are pay scales for certain types of employees such as state minimum wage requirements that cannot be ignored in the hiring of new personnel.

Purchasing

Public and private institutions have regulations regarding purchasing goods and services. For many public institutions, purchasing goods and services can be complicated by mandatory state contracts for certain goods and services at all state agencies, including public colleges or universities. When a state contract is in place for a certain product, the unit budget manager must show cause not to purchase from that source. State bidding laws vary from state to state by low-bid requirements sometimes requiring institutions to purchase something when another product might better meet their needs. Thus when contract criteria are decided upon, institutional personnel should try their best to have their input considered in the development of such language.

An additional complication occurs when a state has a mandatory requirement that all state agencies adhere to low bids on all state contracts. Unless the bidding language is very precise, the result can sometimes be the selection of a vendor or product that is inferior or does not meet the requirements of an institution of higher education.

Usually at private institutions, purchasing requirements are less rigid and are not complicated by blanket state contracts. In fact, purchasing for many items is highly decentralized in a private institution, with the unit taking responsibility for seeking bids and making decisions on the purchase. Whereas on the surface such freedom can seem very attractive, it also requires that each person responsible for the budget exercise due diligence in managing the resources of the institution under his or her control.

Audit Requirements

Audit requirements exist for both private and public institutions. An external audit provides an independent review of the decisions made in a unit or department. Such audits can be costly and have financial implications for the institution or sometimes the budget unit being audited. Both financial and management reports are issued when an audit occurs. After review the responsible persons in the department agree to needed changes in unit policies and procedures in order to comply with the audit findings. A regular follow-up is then conducted to assure that the needed changes have been adopted.

In some public or private institutions there is an internal audit office that regularly conducts audits of all departments of the institution. If an administrator is lucky enough to be in such an institution, use of the internal audit office can strengthen budgetary and procedural oversight within the institution. As a new manager, it is a good practice to ask the internal audit office to conduct an audit of the unit to identify problems or weaknesses in financial and budgetary procedures. In other institutions, audits are conducted by an outside firm. Whatever the process, good auditing can strengthen the financial management of a budget unit.

Public institutions encounter the added complication of audits from the state level. For example, in Illinois the auditor general is required by law to regularly conduct audits of all state agencies, including public colleges and universities. The audit findings are then issued to the institution or unit within the institution, and a written public response must be made to any negative audit finding. A negative audit finding by the state agency can be a source of institutional embarrassment since it is a very public record.

The Role of a Budget Manager

Budgets and financial matters never seem to be topics that stir the souls of individual program managers, department heads, or other administrative staff. However, mastering the skills involved in budget management and understanding the budgetary processes of the institution are essential for success as a vice president, dean, department chair, director, assistant director, or other administrative or management position. Good managers in higher education have a primary role of garnering the resources needed to implement the ideas, programs, and services needed to meet the educational mission of the institution and the unit. Depending on the function of the budgetary unit this could mean having sufficient resources to provide the classes and instruction required, the equipment needs for laboratories or research projects, or services and programs for students. It is not enough, however, to merely obtain money to support the unit. Those with budget responsibility as part of their job responsibilities must assure that those resources are spent in accordance with institutional policies and all applicable statutes. For unit goals and objectives to be reached the needed human and fiscal resources must be in place, and that requires the individual with budget management responsibilities to master budgeting and financial processes and procedures.

The organization of each institution of higher education is unique. Some complex institutions have an elaborate organization with many program and administrative units and many layers of authority for decision making and financial management. Other institutions are organized in a less complex fashion. No matter what the organization of the institution or the specific title of the unit budget manager (program manager, director, chair, assistant or associate dean, dean, assistant or associate vice president, or vice president), the role of the person with budget management responsibility is very consistent. That person must make sound fiduciary judgments, be an informed listener, be adept in gathering fiscal resources, be an institutional friend maker, and be a fiscal problem solver for the unit.

Sound Fiduciary Judgments

The financial success of the institution is highly dependent on each person with budget management responsibilities consistently making sound fiduciary judgments. Those decisions must be made every day for both big and small expenditures. A budget manager often is faced with pressures to do what is easiest or most expedient, but being a sound and honest budget manager requires constant attention to detail and to policies and procedures. In addition, an effective budget manager, at all levels, must follow institutional fiscal policies, meet deadlines, and solve problems before they become major concerns to the institution or the unit. Sound and consistent fiscal management is an essential first step toward general management effectiveness.

Informed Listener

A second, but less recognized role of a person with budget management responsibility is that of an informed listener for the institution. It is often the departmental person managing the budget who hears of issues and problems influencing employee morale or their ability to get their work done. For example, it is usually someone in an administrative or academic department who experiences a problem with a new purchasing or human resource data system that has been installed. If that person just assumes that those responsible for maintaining the system knows of the problem rather than reporting it to them, things will not get any better. The wise administrator with budget management responsibilities will convey specific concerns to those who can address the problem and offer to partner with others in an improvement effort. Such partnerships could include offering to provide test purchase orders so that the specific problem can be identified or specifically demonstrating the problems he or she has experienced trying to get a newly hired staff member into the human resources data system. The time and energy involved with such problem-solving partnerships is well worth the effort and reduces frustration for everyone involved.

Resource Gathering

A third function of a person with budget management responsibilities focuses on resource gathering through fundraising. Requests for outside funding should always be coordinated through the appropriate institutional office, and if a young and eager colleague fails to do so, the wise budget administrator helps the colleague mend needed relationships while fixing the problem. In addition, the unit budget manager can gather resources by partnering with other units in the purchase of major equipment that might be shared or by covering vacation absences of clerical staff through sharing part-time personnel between two departments. Creative budget management requires thinking beyond the usual solutions to issues.

Friend Making

Budget management also involves serving as a friend maker for the institution in their interactions with vendors and members of the public. One development officer noted in a casual conversation that everyone in the institution has the potential to be a friend maker for the institution but that they rarely recognize their responsibility to do so. Helping staff members within the units understand and appreciate this important role is an essential responsibility of a budget manager.

Fiscal Problem Solver

Finally, those with budget management responsibilities are also the problem solver for the unit when it comes to fiscal issues. Helping colleagues figure out how to approach a problem and achieve an optimal solution is a critical skill that helps any budget unit achieve success. In order to fulfill this role, budget managers must develop a web of helping relationships and partnerships across the campus. Understanding who to call under what circumstances is a prime function of anyone with fiscal responsibilities. To be a good steward of fiscal resources requires much more than knowledge of money and balance sheets, although such a firm knowledge base certainly helps.

Why Does All This Matter?

Understanding the broader fiscal context for higher education is a first step in becoming an effective budget manager for a unit. No budget or program in an institution of higher education stands alone. The budget requests for one unit may have implications for another. To illustrate, the person who has budget responsibilities for the learning disabilities center sees a quick solution to the need for more money to provide additional services to students: charge students for screening tests that up to this time were offered without charge. This approach to solving a budget dilemma has ramifications beyond the learning disabilities clinic. A fee-for-services approach might, for example, influence the financial aid budget or the athletic budget or there may be legal implications for the institution. When it comes to money unilateral decisions should not be made by one part of the institution as doing so risks unexpected consequences.

It is true that many similarities exist between the fiscal realities faced by private and public institutions of higher education. However, there are also differences. Understanding those differences and the unique policies and procedures related to institutional type will help anyone with budget responsibilities be more effective. For example, most public institutions are concerned with the growth of their workforce, and new positions are subject to a rigorous review process. As a budget manager you may even have the money to create the new position, but you may not have the authority to hire for a new position without approvals elsewhere in the institution or at the state level. In a well-endowed private institution, however, the concern is to control total expenditures and not just positions. The essential point is that those with budget management responsibilities must understand the important funding priorities for their institution, the sources of funds, and the budgetary procedures of their institution.

Alpha University

Alpha University has been created to illustrate the complexity of budget decisions at any university. It will be referred to throughout this volume. The following case study, involving a budget surplus, illustrates what institutions must confront when making budget decisions.

Case Study: Bountiful Times at Alpha University

Alpha University is a midsized public institution in a state where institutions receive some support from the state (which varies from year to year), has a modest endowment, is dependent on mandatory fees to provide many student services (recreation, intercollegiate athletics, health service), is able to retain the tuition revenue at the local level that is generated through enrollment, and has a modest research program that has been remarkably successful.

A combination of factors has resulted in increased revenue to the institution of approximately $10 million for the next fiscal year. The increase in revenue is the result of a modest increase in tuition, new charges for the rental of facilities to outside groups, modest enrollment growth at the undergraduate level, two bequests which endowed faculty positions in English and in chemistry, providing budget relief for the institution, a 2% increase in state funding, an increase in mandatory student fees and room and board costs, and a modest growth in research grants resulting in an increase in indirect cost reimbursement to the institution. The result is a net increase of $10 million to the institution.

The university budget committee has received budget increase requests totaling more than $14 million dollars for the next fiscal year. Although it is clear that all such requests cannot be funded, the question of how to allocate the new revenue is much more complex than simply denying funding to $4 million of requests. Issues that influence the allocation of the $10 million in additional revenue include the following:

- There is a governing board policy that requires that any increase in tuition and fees must result in a proportional increase in the student financial aid budget (estimated cost: $1 million).

- The faculty and staff are expecting at least a 3.5% salary increment for the next fiscal year (estimated cost: $2.8 million).

- Health insurance costs have skyrocketed, resulting in a premium increase for the next fiscal year (estimated cost for the institutional share: $650,000).

- After a Title IX complaint an agreed upon plan with the Office of Civil Rights involves an increase in support for women's intercollegiate athletics (estimated cost: $450,000 in the first year, $300,000 a year thereafter).

- New faculty must be hired for the next academic year to cover the increased demand for required core courses. There has been an increase in student complaints regarding their inability to get into needed core courses in a timely manner, and inquiries have come from parents and legislators (estimated cost: $750,000 in the base budget).

- An unanticipated increase in postal rates has resulted in an increase in the total institutional base budget for postage (estimated cost: $27,000).

- The first phase of a three-year upgrade of the network and supporting software must begin in the next fiscal year (estimated cost: $1,500,000 each year).

- The counseling center has a long waiting list and is requesting two additional positions for the regular academic year and one for the entire fiscal year (estimated cost including benefits and increased malpractice premiums: $270,000).

- The governing board would like to attract more National Merit Scholars and has strongly suggested that the institution present a budget with a substantial increase in the institutional base budget for that purpose (estimated cost: $500,000 per year).

- The cost of natural gas is rising, resulting in an institutional budget increase for the next fiscal year (estimated cost: $400,000).

Additional requests have been received as follows:

1. A five-year program of installation of programmable thermo-stats in all academic buildings to reduce heating costs at night and the weekend (estimated cost: $250,000—would pay for itself in five years).

2. New lab equipment in the department of chemistry (estimated cost: $200,000).

3. New furniture for the student center lounge, which has not been replaced since the building opened 15 years ago (esti-mated cost: $550,000).

4. Resurfacing of parking lots in the north campus (estimated cost: $250,000).

5. The establishment of a center to improve writing for students at the undergraduate and graduate levels (estimated cost for reconstruction of space and hiring of staff: $1.7 million).

6. Addition of a new master's degree program in integrated man-agement (estimated cost: $1 million—estimated to pay for itself in six years).

7. Reconstruction of interview space in the Career Planning and Placement area (estimated cost: $400,000).

8. Establishment of a freshman seminar program for all enter-ing first-year students regardless of major (estimated cost: $825,000).

9. Development of a strong alumni network for career planning (estimated cost: $100,000).

10. Adding two intramural playing fields with lights on undevel-oped land (estimated cost: $1.2 million).

11. Development of a childcare support program for faculty, staff, and students (estimated cost: $750,000).

The task of the budget committee is to make recommenda-tions to the president regarding what budget requests should be approved for the next year. For this year only capital requests and general operating requests are being considered together because of the additional available revenue. As members of the committee you must decide what recommendations to make to the president. As part of those recommendations you must identify:

1. The mandated increases that *must* be funded.
2. A priority list of other budget requests with justifications for those requests.

References

American Association of State Colleges and Universities State Relations and Policy Analysis Research Team. *Top Ten State Policy Issues for Higher Education. In 2009. AASCU Policy Matters, A Higher Education Policy Brief*, January 2009.

Association of Research Libraries. *ARL Statistics 2003–04*. Washington, D.C.: Association of Research Libraries, 2005. Accessed on May 2, 2010, at http://www.arl.org/bm~doc/arlstat04.pdf.

Callan, P., and Finney, J. (eds.). *Public and Private Financing of Higher Education: Shaping Public Policy for the Future*. Washington, D.C.: American Council on Education/Oryx Press, 1997.

Goldstein, L. *College and University Budgeting*. National Association of College and University Business Officers: Washington, D.C., 2005.

Harvey, J. *Straight Talk About College Costs and Prices: The Report of the National Commission on the Cost of Higher Education*. American Institutes for Research: Washington, D.C., 1998.

Immerwahr, J., and Foleno, T. *Great Expectations: How the Public and Parents—White, African-American and Hispanic—View Higher Education*. San Jose: National Center for Public Policy and Higher Education, May 2000 (pp. 33–34).

Lingenfelter, P. (et. al) *State Higher Education Finance. FY2003*. Denver, CO: State Higher Education Executive Officers, 2004.

National Center for Educational Statistics, Sources of Funds, Public College and Universities, etc. Washington, D.C.: U.S. Department of Education, 2008. Accessed on January 6, 2010, at http://nces.ed.gov/programs/digest/d08/figures/fig_16.asp?referrer=list and http://nces.ed.gov/programs/digest/d08/figures/fig_17.asp?referrer=list

Schuh, J. "Fiscal Pressures on Higher Education and Student Affairs." In
    M. J. Barr and M.K. Desler (eds.), *The Handbook of Student Affairs
    Administration*. San Francisco: Jossey-Bass, 2000.
Zhu, P. "Harvard Endowment, Largest in Higher Education Plummets." *The
    Harvard Crimson*, September 19, 2009.

Reflection Questions

1. What constraints from the larger environment will influence the daily work of your unit?

2. What are the potential opportunities for your unit because of events and decisions within the larger environment?

3. Is your unit responsible for responding to unfunded federal and state mandates? If so, what are the budget implications for this fiscal year and beyond?

4. As you set priorities what criteria should you use in doing so?

5. What budget choices are one-time only and what choices would lead to multi-year obligations for the institution?

6. What political or other internal campus dynamics will influence the committee recommendation?

Primary Elements of the Budget

Revenue and Expenses

In Chapter One we discussed the role of the budget manager across the broad spectrum of administrative units, academic departments, and institutional types in higher education. We also discussed budgetary challenges in the context of contemporary practice. In this chapter we consider the two primary elements of any budget—revenues and expenses. We use examples of budget statements throughout the chapter to illustrate the information shared. The relationship between revenues and expenses and the relationship between both and institutional mission and strategic plan will be addressed in Chapter Three.

Revenues

A number of revenue sources support both public and private (independent) institutions of higher education. This section provides a description of the common sources of revenue. The emphasis and dependence on each source of financial support will vary between institutions even of the same type. However, as noted in Chapter One, the greatest variance in sources of support will occur between public and private institutions.

Some revenues are allocated, collected, or donated for a specific purpose. These are referred to as restricted funds. Restricted funds may be used only for the purposes specified by the source of the funds. Grant funds and money collected from designated student fees are common examples of restricted revenue funds.

State Appropriated Funds

Funds from the state government are the primary source of income for most public colleges and universities. At a public community college such income may also be supplemented by direct support from the county or municipality in which the institution is located.

The processes involved in allocating state funds to a public institution of higher education will differ in each state. Some states use a formula to determine the base funding level for institutions (see Chapter Three for a more extensive treatment of formula budgeting). In still other states, legislative review of the institutional budget is extensive and may involve line item review of all budget items. Finally, a limited number of institutions, such as the University of Michigan, are constitutionally autonomous (not subject to regulation by other state agencies) and thus are treated in the legislative budget process, as is any other state agency.

The role of state appropriations for private institutions is much narrower than within the public sector. State appropriations for private institutions are usually limited to specific programs that meet state priorities and interests. This might include, for example, support for medical education, teacher education, or programs that prepare graduates to work with persons with disabilities. In addition, state support for private institutions may come in the form of capital budget support (see Chapter Three) or through direct financial grants to students.

Tuition

Undergraduate tuition is the engine that drives much of higher education in the private sector and is becoming more important in the public sector. The states of Vermont and Virginia provide excellent examples of this trend. In those states, the flagship public institutions do not rely on state appropriations as the main support for the operating budget.

The price of tuition at both public and private institutions can be calculated on the basis of each credit hour taken or on a full-time enrollment basis. In this age of increased consumerism, many institutions are abandoning the practice of charging for each credit hour to avoid student and parental complaints such as "I spent X dollars on that course and did not learn anything and I want my money back." Bundling tuition into full-time and part-time charges also eliminates refunds if a student drops a course prior to the end of the add/drop period.

Tuition at public institutions may be set by their governing board, by state commission, or by the state legislature depending upon the laws of that state. Public institutions often have statutory restrictions regarding the amount of tuition that may be charged to in-state residents. The rationale for such restrictions is the fact that the state already allocates money to the institution, and citizens of the state should not have to pay an exorbitant amount in order to attend "their" state college or university. Usually there are not such restrictions on out-of-state tuition, and the institution or system may be free to charge (with appropriate approvals) whatever the traffic will bear. Artificial restrictions on the amount of in-state tuition that can be charged create unique fiscal challenges for state institutions, and many are seeking legislative relief on tuition caps in order to adequately fund the enterprise.

In private institutions, tuition is a critical component of the institutional budget. Tuition in private institutions is set by the governing board and is carefully calculated in comparison to other private institutions, which are in direct competition with the institution. In smaller or struggling institutions, enrollment (and thus tuition dollars) can be the difference between meeting the revenue needed to support the operating budget of the institution and failing to do so.

Graduate tuition, whether it is paid by the student from a grant or through a tuition waiver program linked to an assistantship, does not begin to pay the cost for graduate education. Exceptions to this rule include specialized master's degree programs offered on a part-time basis to full-tuition-paying students and the small but growing number of graduate certificate programs also typically offered on a part-time basis to full-tuition-paying students. Doctoral programs usually are costly to the institution and are only rarely offset by direct tuition payments or grant support. Professional school programs also provide similar budgetary challenges for the institution, although there are certainly some MBA programs that do pay their way. Graduate programs are essential in a research or comprehensive institution because they attract top-flight faculty and students and because of their role in expanding knowledge. However, in the fiscal sense, they are not moneymakers or major contributors to the funding stream for any institutional budget.

Mandatory Student Fees

At public institutions (and increasingly at private colleges and universities) student fees earmarked for a specific purpose have been seen as a way to obtain revenue without raising tuition. In the highly politicized context for higher education, imposition of student fees is seen as a way to avoid confrontations on the issue of tuition cost. Such fees are usually charged on a term basis to full-time undergraduate students and may also be charged to students in graduate or professional programs. Examples include building use fees, technology fees, bond revenue fees, recreation fees, laboratory fees, breakage fees, student services fees, health service fees, and student activity fees. Mandatory fees are usually dedicated as support for a specific building or program and must be reserved only for those purposes. For example, a steady stream from a mandatory student recreation fee is often the fiscal foundation for construction of student recreation buildings. Or technology fees are reserved to support the maintenance of the wireless network on campus.

The process of allocating mandatory student fees varies from institution to institution. In some institutions, mandatory fees are routinely allocated to support units as part of the general budget process. In others, a committee with student representation allocates the fees for use by departments and programs. In many cases, mandatory student activity fees are solely allocated by student government structures under the general supervision of an administrative unit.

In the past, private institutions were much less likely to adopt the strategy of mandatory student fees as a means to generate income. Many of the programs and services at public institutions that are supported by such general student fees are funded by more robust tuition income at private institutions. That philosophy may be changing as public concern has grown about the rising cost of tuition at private institutions, and it is likely that more fees for individual programs will be found in private institutions.

Endowment Income

Income from the investment of the institutional endowment is often a significant source of support for private institutions. Overall fiduciary responsibility for managing endowment investments rests with the institutional governing board at private institutions. Day-by-day management issues are the responsibility of institutional staff or outside investment firms. The income from the investment of the endowment is used to support the yearly operating budget of the institution.

Currently, most major public institutions have much more modest endowments than their private counterparts. That is likely to change as state-appropriated support for public higher education diminishes and alternative sources of revenue are needed. Whereas in private institutions the endowment is under the control of the governing board, that is not necessarily the case in public institutions. At some public institutions independent foundations have been established to raise money and invest for the good of the institution. Any such foundation must meet the requirements of state statutes and state regulations in the state where the foundation is located. The organization and control of such independent foundations will vary. For example, some have institutional representatives on their governing board and some do not. Some are absolutely independent, and some receive office space as well as clerical and accounting support from the institution. Each situation is unique and often is dependent on the history and tradition of the institution. Independent foundations create tremendous management challenges for an institutional chief executive. In such cases, the CEO does not control a critical source of funds to support the enterprise.

Prudent institutions do not use all of the income generated by investing the endowment for current operations. Instead, rules are established by the governing board regarding the percentage of the endowment income that may be spent on operations for any fiscal year. The remaining income from endowment investments is reinvested in the corpus of the endowment, thus allowing it to grow. Such spending limits also create a more stable revenue stream for the institution, as it is not buffeted as much by the winds of change in a fluctuating economy. It also provides discipline to the institutional budgeting process by not having the operating budget of the institution become so dependent on endowment income that a market downturn would cause disruption of the educational activities of the institution. Although most institutions pursue conservative policies with respect to the percentage of revenue from their endowment used to fund the operating budget (Ernst & Young LLP, 2009), there have been notable exceptions in recent years even among some institutions thought of as being among the most well managed. Harvard, Dartmouth, and Stanford are among those whose heavy reliance on endowment income to fund operating budgets proved particularly problematic in difficult economic times (Masterson, 2008a, 2008b; Staley, 2009).

Endowment income can either be part of the central budget allocation to the unit or in some cases departments or units have endowment funds specifically dedicated for support of unit programs and activities. In the latter case, the income from dedicated endowments can be subject to the same spending rules as for the total endowment and cannot be spent on other institutional activities.

How large should an endowment be in order to assure the fiscal health of the private institution? Each institution is unique, and that question will depend on a number of factors, including the dependence of the institution on the endowment for annual operating funds. One way to measure the strength of the endowment is to examine it in terms of student enrollment. Divide the student enrollment into the endowment and determine what the endowment support is for each student. If the result of that exercise is a high number, the institution certainly has a strong endowment foundation.

Many institutions, both public and private, have limited endowment funds and some do not have any such support. Without substantial endowment support, an institution may be in a state of constant uncertainty regarding the fiscal future, and planning and institutional growth are thwarted.

Special Student Fees

There are two types of special student fees used to support budget expenditures: one-time fees and fees for services. Both types of special use student fees are present in both public and private institutions.

One-time fees are assessed for participation in a specific program or activity. Examples of one-time fees include first year experience, study abroad fees, loan processing fees, and commencement fees. The income from the fees helps to offset the cost of the specific program without causing a drain on other institutional resources.

Fees for services are a growing phenomenon in higher education and are usually linked to psychological services, health care, or the ability for students to attend popular intercollegiate athletic events. To illustrate, in many counseling centers students seeking help are provided a limited number of counseling sessions at no cost but must provide some form of co-payment to continue therapy once all free services have been used. Debate has occurred regarding whether students should be charged in this manner, as often those who need the service the most are the least likely to be able to pay. While the debate continues, the fee-for-services approach to meeting revenue needs continues to expand.

Student fees have also been a source of support for popular athletic programs. Usually a separate athletic fee is optional for undergraduate students. Students paying the athletic fee are able to access tickets to football or basketball games and at least are able to participate in a lottery for tickets if the institution's team goes to a bowl or a post-season tournament.

Gifts

Identifying and obtaining private financial support from alumni, friends, parents, business, industry, and foundations is essential to the fiscal health of private institutions and is becoming increasingly important at public institutions. There are three types of fundraising that characterize this process at most institutions: annual giving, focused giving for a specific project (including capital campaigns), and long-term campaigns for broad institutional priorities and projects.

Annual Giving

For most private institutions, annual giving is a critical revenue source for the operating budget of the institution. Revenue goals are set for the development staff of the institution based on past performance, market conditions, and inflation. Those charged with responsibility for raising the target dollars for the annual fund then develop fundraising strategies that have worked in their particular institution. Former donors are contacted, research is done on new donors, and interests of potential donors are carefully catalogued even if the potential donor does not give this year. Thus a database is built for future solicitations and support for specific programs and services. For the most part annual fund donors designate their contributions to broad areas of need at the institution such as libraries, financial aid, and the like. Once in awhile donors dedicate some annual gifts for specific units or programs. Such gifts, while welcome, are not usually incremental to the unit but replace institutional allocations in the budget process. When a gift is not dedicated it becomes part of the general revenue stream for the institution. Establishment of a robust annual giving program is essential to the financial health of most private institutions of higher education.

Campaigns

To meet the needs for new facilities or new program initiatives many institutions conduct multiyear campaigns. In recent years such campaigns have evidenced a greater emphasis on program support as opposed to "bricks and mortar" capital campaigns. Included in such initiatives are undergraduate scholarship programs, graduate fellowships, endowed chairs and professorships, and specific endowments to support specialized programs such as centers for the study of humanities.

Still other institutions raise funds for specific programs and needs as opposed to a comprehensive campaign. This more precise form of fundraising relies on in-depth knowledge of donor interests and compatibility of those interests with institutional needs.

Whatever the approach to fundraising adopted by an institution, it is clear that fundraising on both an annual and long-term basis is becoming more important to both public and private institutions. It is tempting to accept any and all gifts offered to the institution, but astute administrators must examine whether the gift will be additive or will, in the long run, cost the institution more than the initial gift. There is an old adage in fundraising: "Beware of the gift that eats."

Finally, institutionwide coordination of fundraising activities is essential, for it is not in the best interest of the institution for potential donors to be approached by several institutional units at the same time. It is essential that someone be in charge of what requests are being made in the name of the institution and assure that the success with small requests does not eliminate potential larger donations.

Grants and Contracts

Research at colleges and universities is supported in large part through grants from the federal government, state agencies, business and industry, and private foundations. In addition to providing direct support in terms of salaries and operating costs for the specific research activity, grants also are required to recapture the indirect costs (sometimes called the facilities and administration costs) of the institution related to the grant. Indirect costs include, for example, services provided by the institution such as accounting and purchasing, utilities, space, and administration. The indirect cost rate of the federal government is based on a calculation developed by the Office of Management and Budget (OMB Circular 21-A). However, the trend has been for there to be a growing list of expenditures for which the government prohibits or caps recovery of indirect costs. The problem of recouping the costs from the federal government for grants is further complicated by the additional requirements of the Cost Accounting Standards Board (CASB). Grants, though a source of funding, are also a source of headaches for most administrators with financial oversight of grants as part of their budget portfolio (Goldstein, 2005). Federal and state reimbursements for indirect costs do not accrue in the unit budget in which the grant is lodged but are instead part of the general revenue stream in support of the institution.

Contracts are time-limited arrangements with business, industry, or government whereby the institution provides a direct service in return for a payment. Examples of contracts entered into by colleges and universities include providing training for personnel in a state agency, teaching an academic course for the employees of a specific company, or providing technical computer support for local government. Such contracts usually include an overhead line that covers some of the same costs that the indirect cost rate noted above does. The institution establishes the over-head rate for all such contracts and the money is returned for the general use of the institution.

Most institutions have centralized approval processes for both grants and contracts. Such centralization assures that agreement to the terms of the contract by authorized institutional person-nel has been given. In addition, calculations for indirect costs, salaries, and benefits can be checked for accuracy. If the pro-posed contract or grant receives funding, the centralized grants and contracts office supervises fund disbursement and supervises reporting requirements of the grant or contract. Thus, the first step in developing a proposal for an outside grant or contract is contact with the office in charge of such activities.

Auxiliary Services

Auxiliary units usually do not receive any institutional support and are expected to generate sufficient income to cover all operat-ing expenses and long-term facility costs associated with the unit. In addition to meeting all expenses and long-term facility needs auxiliary enterprises are also expected to pay overhead to the institution to cover the costs of institutional services (similar to grants) used by the auxiliary unit. Examples of auxiliary services include student housing, food service, student unions, recreation programs, and at times intercollegiate athletics. Chapter Five in this volume provides an in-depth discussion of auxiliary units and the unique budget opportunities and challenges that they present to any administrator.

Special Programs

A special program may be a one-time event such as a department-sponsored conference for which entrance or registration fees are charged or a recurring program such as a sports camp that occurs every summer. In either case, the program must be self-supporting unless specific institutional permission has been granted to allow expenses to exceed income. Revenue generated by the event is usually retained by the sponsoring unit to offset expenses. The budgetary goal of the event is to break even at the end of the year. Modest reserve funds may be established for such programs in order to deal with a year when expenses are higher than revenue. If this happens on a continuing basis, however, review of the pricing policies associated with the program may occur or the efficacy of the program may be questioned by institutional administrators. Before any plans are made or implemented for a special program, appropriate administrative approval must be received for the venture.

Contracted Institutional Services

In both public and private institutions, services such as bookstores, food service, custodial services, vending machines, and washers and dryers are increasingly being outsourced through contracts with private enterprise. Through a competitive bidding process such contracts can become a source of funds to support both operations and capital expenditures such as facility repair, renovation, and new construction. Negotiation of those contracts may include a yearly lump sum payment for capital expenses in addition to regular payments to the institution based on a percentage of gross sales.

The concept of contracted institutional services has been expanded on some campuses to include exclusive use contracts for soft drinks or other merchandise on campus. Under such contracts the entire institution adopts a certain brand of soft drink (or athletic equipment supplier, vending machine operator, telephone service, or food service management company) and for that exclusive market the company makes lump sum payments each year to the institution in addition to contract obligation of a percentage of gross sales.

Any contracts for institutional services should be reviewed by institutional legal counsel because the contract commits the institution to certain actions. In addition, the individual signing the contract on behalf of the institution must have clear authority to do so. Finally, supervision of the contract to assure vendor compliance with contract expectations must occur.

Hospitals

Some universities operate teaching hospitals. Because of the relative scarcity of these organizations and the complexity of their budgets, discussion of hospitals in this chapter is limited to simply acknowledging them as a special case.

Licensing, Patents, and Royalties

Like all corporate entities, universities have the right to control the use of their image as conveyed in their name or recognized imagery. Universities capitalize on their images through the licensing of products bearing their image. Examples include sportswear, license plates, household goods (such as blankets or waste cans), class rings, diploma frames, and more. The licensing contract typically spells out the specific products for which a license is granted, the territory for which the license is granted (regional, national, or international), the period of time for which the license is granted and terms for subsequent renewals of the license, and the extent to which the license is or is not exclusive. In return, the contract provides for the institution to receive a percentage of the sales of the licensed products bearing the institution's name, crest, logos, or other recognized imagery.

It is increasingly common for university contracts with faculty and staff to address the issue of intellectual property rights regarding work done while at the university. Through those contracts institutions establish ownership positions in the creative product of work done while at the university. Hence, they receive some portion of the revenue generated through the patents, licensing, or royalties associated with the product. When Northwestern University sold a portion of its future royalty proceeds from Lyrica, Dr. Richard Silverman, a professor in chemistry whose work while at the university was crucial to the development of the drug, and Ryszard Andruszkiewicz, who served as Dr. Silverman's postdoc student, both received a share of the proceeds (Blumenstyk, 2007).

Church Support

Church-supported or church-related private institutions of higher education also rely on denominational financial support either through endowments or contributions to the annual fund. Such support usually carries with it a requirement for representation on the governing board of the institution and assurances that the values of the religious groups will be upheld through institutional policies and programs. As religious groups, of all kinds, face reduced membership the amount of direct denominational support as a proportion of the institutional budget for church-related institutions has diminished.

Other Sources of Income

There are a number of miscellaneous sources of income used to support facilities and programs in American higher education. Facility rental fees, charged to outside groups, help offset the operating costs of large concert halls and other performance venues. The privilege of parking on campus requires parking permits which all eligible community members must purchase. Parking fines are used to support enforcement of the parking program, and library fines are used for library operations. Rental fees for specialized pieces of equipment such as stadium field coverings are but one example of the creative way institutional budget managers generate income to support programs. Although individually such sources of support seem to be small in relation to the institutional budget, in the aggregate such income sources are critical to the financial health of the institution.

During the recession that began in 2008 many institutions benefitted from the receipt of federally appropriated State Fiscal Stabilization Funds (SFSF) included in the American Recovery and Reinvestment Act of 2009. Funding from the SFSF flowed to institutions through the states in which they were located, and in at least some instances SFSF program resources promised to institutions early in the recession were withheld by states, for the purposes of stabilizing eroding state budgets, as the recession worsened. The SFSF program was limited to providing one-time (or non-recurring) infusion of resources.

State Capital Budgets

In some states capital development funds for new facilities or facility renovation at public institutions are funded through a budget process separate from that of the operating budget of the institution. Capital support for facilities can be requested through a process that is in addition to the regular appropriation process. Usually, those funds are limited, and only facilities that meet the highest priorities of the state higher education coordinating board are funded. Under unusual circumstances private institutions may also be able to access state capital funds if the facility or the program it supports meets a pressing state need.

Federal Capital Support

If proposed new construction supports a federal need and if there is support in the federal appropriations process, then federal dollars may also be available to institutions for a capital construction process. Such federal support is often critical to the successful construction of expensive and complicated research and medical facilities.

———————

It has been argued that higher education, at least in the not-for-profit sector, has an insatiable appetite for revenue, as the only limit on what they can and will spend on what they see as intrinsically worthwhile programs and services is that amount of revenue they can generate (Bowen, 1980). Ehrenberg (2002) described universities as acting like cookie monsters, and Bok (2003) likened them to compulsive gamblers as a result of their seemingly insatiable appetite for revenues to feed expenditures.

Expenditures

Expenditures by higher education institutions in the United States approached $400 billion in 2007–08 (National Center for Education Statistics, 2008) with approximately two-thirds of that amount being spent by public institutions. Whereas there are some notable differences between the sources of revenue between public and private higher education, the two are much more similar when it comes to expenditures.

This section of the chapter offers brief descriptions of expenses commonly found in the budgets of higher education institutions. It is important for budget managers to pay heed to whether the funds that support a particular expenditure have been provided on a restricted or unrestricted basis. There may be times when portions of the expense budget are identified as being for a specific purpose. These funds are then known as designated funds.

Salaries

Salaries are the single largest expense in the budget of any higher education institution. Salary expenses usually are organized by employee category: faculty, exempt or professional staff, nonexempt or support staff, technical or maintenance staff, or student staff.

The budgeted wages and benefits of nonstudent employees are typically reflected as encumbrances on budget statements. Encumbrances represent financial commitments made for which the actual expenditures have yet to take place. Changes in staffing at midyear can result in reductions in encumbrances, thus leading to uncommitted balances in salary wage lines for a particular fiscal year. Such balances are sometimes referred to as "breakage." Although salary dollars are typically not fungible (meaning that funds budgeted on a recurring basis for salaries for authorized faculty or staff positions may not be reallocated to recurring funds budgeted for travel, for example), some institutions permit salary breakage in a given year to be used for one-time nonsalary expenditures in that fiscal year. Breakage can also occur when funds for student employment are underutilized, though such funds are typically not allocated as recurring dollars.

Benefits

Expenses for benefits are a function of expenses for salaries with some set percentage of the salary serving as the basis for calculation of the budgeted benefits at the unit level. Actual institutional expenditures for benefits are typically handled centrally with the unit level benefits budgets being transferred to the central fund monthly or at closing. In this way the institution can manage the variations that occur from year to year in actual benefits at the unit level due to changes in the coverage for particular employees. For example, Alpha University instructed units to budget benefits for the current year at 38% of salary. The Student Life salary budget for the year was set at $200,000, which resulted in $76,000 being budgeted for benefits. It turns out that Student Life staff benefits actually came at a cost of $85,000 due to the addition of a new family member to the benefits package of one employee and the decision by another to elect for a dental plan that the university helps subsidize as a benefit. The result is a $9,000 deficit in the benefits budget line for Student Life. How will that be handled? Like many institutions, Alpha University assumes that actual expenses for benefits will be over in some units and under in others. The unused balances in units' benefits budgets are rolled at closing into a central budget, and those funds are used to cover the shortfall in other units. In years in which the actual expenditure for benefits for all units combined at Alpha University comes in under the budget assumption, the excess is rolled into a reserve account that carries a balance from fiscal year to fiscal year. In years in which overall benefits expenses exceed the budgeted average, Alpha draws on the funds in the benefits reserve account to manage the shortfall.

Program Supplies

Program supplies can include a wide range of expenses. In some units it could include expenditures for lab equipment. Other units might purchase materials for set design. Still others could budget for the purchase of screws, nuts, and washers. Perhaps the most significant example of program supplies would be the budget for acquisitions in an institution's library. A budget may include subcategories for line items. In the case of acquisition for the library, an institution may elect to distinguish between books, periodicals, and other collections.

Office Supplies

Like program supplies, office supplies can include expenditures for a wide array of items ranging from paper to printer cartridges. Institutions often have purchasing arrangements with various vendors for such supplies in order to capitalize on the volume of purchases across the institution. In some instances those arrangements may call for an exclusive relationship in which case all units in the institution are expected to restrict their purchases for the specified supplies to that vendor.

Computer Equipment and Software

The pace of change in information technology is dramatic, and the temptation to buy the latest model can be strong. A prudent budget manager recognizes the difference between wants and needs when it comes to both hardware and software purchases and includes in the budget a plan for periodic replacement of the former and upgrades of the latter.

Communications

Telephone and data lines and usage charges are traditional communication expense items. Budget managers should regularly review recurring line charges for phone and data to assure that the lines are active, necessary, and charged to the appropriate unit. Some institutions host toll-free lines for incoming calls, and others make use of various discounting options in order to control costs for outgoing international calls. In contemporary practice communications expenses frequently include purchase, service contracts, and usage fees for PDAs (personal digital assistants).

Publications and Printing

Despite the growing use of computer mediated communication and social networking resources, higher education still relies heavily on printed materials in the course of doing business. The preparation and printing of everything from recruitment brochures to institutional strategic plans needs to be accounted for in expense budgets. Some items such as student handbooks or commencement programs are annual costs. Others, such as strategic plans, are periodic expenditures, and items such as announcements of presidential inaugurations are one-time or occasional expenses.

Larger institutions may have in-house publications departments to assist units in the development of materials. Expenses for those services may be absorbed centrally or charged off to units on a project basis. Institutions without internal publications assistance may find the costs of professional assistance in developing publications to be daunting. One alternative is to identify and employ students with talent in graphic design or marketing to assist with the project.

Postage

A unit's budget for postage can be very modest or very substantial depending on its mission. The office of the associate vice chancellor for enrollment management at Alpha University has a small postage budget, as most of its communications are internal, whereas admissions, one of the units reporting in enrollment management, has a substantial budget for postage to support national and international recruitment mailings. Smaller institutions may elect to centralize expenses for postage rather than go through the expense of supporting the infrastructure necessary to track decentralized costs.

Programming

It is not uncommon for units to have budgeted expenses for programming or programming support. The Anthropology Department with an ongoing noon-time presentation series might have such an expense item. Offices of Multicultural Affairs might budget support for cultural celebrations presented by student organizations. Campus Life might budget for its annual celebration of student leadership.

Budget managers should be careful to understand the true costs associated with particular programs, as some expenses may be subsumed in other budget lines. Although entertainment and equipment fees for Alpha University's annual campuswide spring celebration are reflected in the programming budget of its special events unit in the president's office, there are additional costs for groundskeeping and insurance that are absorbed in the facilities management budget in business affairs.

Both public and private institutions may have policies that restrict the use of institutional funds for certain types of expenditures. Although some are silent on the subject, there are institutions that prohibit or limit expenditures on food, decorations, or awards. Budget managers and program staff must be familiar with such policies where they are in place.

Professional Development

Examples of professional development expenses can include registration fees for webinars, registration fees for conferences, or reimbursement for special courses taken to develop or refresh necessary skills. Unfortunately professional development is one of the expenditure categories most vulnerable to budget cuts during times of fiscal constraints.

Memberships and Periodicals

Institutional dues in associations are a common expense item. Typically professionals are expected to be responsible for their personal dues for association membership. Similarly, institutional subscriptions to professional periodicals are a common expense item whereas individual professionals are typically not reimbursed by institutions for their subscriptions. Non-reimbursed business expenses such as individual association dues or subscriptions to professional periodicals may, however, be tax deductible.

Travel

Budgets for travel expenditures address costs associated with activities such as business meetings, professional conferences, or recruitment trips by admissions or athletics. Specific expenditures can include airfare, ground transportation, and meal allowances (either on the basis of actual receipts or per diem allowances). Most institutions have established policies and procedures for travel. These typically address allowable modes of travel, acceptable hotel accommodations, caps on meal expenses or entertainment, and rates for reimbursement for the use of personal vehicles.

Travel expenses, like professional development expenses with which there is often overlap, constitute another area that comes under considerable scrutiny at times of fiscal constraints. Budget managers would be wise to closely monitor these expenditures to assure compliance with applicable policy as well as to assure that reasonable frugality is the watchword of decision making when it comes to travel.

Entertainment and Gifts

Outside of development offices and executive administrative offices there are very few units that have entertainment and gift expense budgets. Public institutions typically have restrictions regarding the use of public funds for such expenses and so make use of foundation funds to engage in these activities.

Food and beverages are a common form of expense in higher education. Such expenses, like those for entertainment and gifts, are commonly subject to specific policies specifying permissible purposes, costs, and funding sources. Depending on the purpose and institutional practice, food and beverage costs are commonly charged to entertainment, programming, promotion, or professional development budgets.

Facilities

Units may be charged for facilities services such as the changing of locks or the moving of furniture. Budgets should account for these expenses.

Utilities

Utilities are second perhaps only to benefits in the rate at which expenses in higher education are increasing. The price that colleges and universities pay for electricity, water, sewer service, and fuel oil are all rising rapidly. With the exception of charges related to the operation of auxiliary units (see Chapter Five), expenses for utilities are typically handled through an institution's facilities management budget.

Contracted Services

Institutions and units within institutions contract for a host of services. Examples include waste removal, copier maintenance, invited speakers, and janitorial services.

Debt Service

Debt service is an expense category that is typically associated with auxiliary or capital budgets (see Chapter Three). However, some smaller institutions regularly access lines of credit to fund operations pending receipt of tuition revenues and have budgeted expenditures for debt service.

Scholarships and Fellowships

Expenditures for scholarships and fellowships are often offset by tuition revenues received from the recipients of the very same scholarships and fellowships. Good accounting practices require that both the expenditures and the revenues be tracked.

Miscellaneous

Budget managers should be particularly wary of the miscellaneous expense line item. Unless paid careful attention, it can become a catch-all that hinders the accurate reflection of expenses associated with the operation of a unit.

Conclusion

Although there are as many variations on lists of revenue and expenditure types as there are institutions of higher education, this chapter has provided a general overview of many of the most common types of each. One of the most important first duties of an individual becoming responsible for the budget of a unit is to become familiar with that unit's revenues and expenses and the relationship between them and the institutional budget.

References

Blumenstyk, G. "Northwestern U. Sells Royalty Rights from Blockbuster Drug for $700-Million." *The Chronicle of Higher Education*, Dec. 19, 2007.

Bok, D. *Universities in the Marketplace: The Commercialization of Higher Education*. Princeton, NJ: Princeton University Press, 2003.

Bowen, H. R. *The Costs of Higher Education: How Much Do Colleges and Universities Spend Per Student and How Much Should They Spend?* San Francisco: Jossey-Bass, 1980.

Ehrenberg, R. G. *Tuition Rising: Why College Costs So Much*. Cambridge, MA: Harvard University Press, 2002.

Ernst & Young LLP. "2008 Internal Revenue Service Colleges and Universities Compliance Questionnaire Analysis." Washington, D.C.: Association of Governing Boards of Universities, and Colleges and National Association of College and University Business Officers, 2009.

Goldstein, L. *College and University Budgeting: An Introduction for Faculty and Academic Administrators*. Washington D.C.: National Association of College and University Business Officers, 2005.

Masterson, K. "A Sobering Message from Harvard's President." *The Chronicle of Higher Education*, Nov. 21, 2008a.

Masterson, K. "Dartmouth Cuts Budget and Says Layoffs May Be Needed." *The Chronicle of Higher Education*, Nov. 13, 2008b.

National Center for Education Statistics. *Digest of Education Statistics: 2008*. Washington, DC: Department of Education, 2008. Accessed on November 21, 2009, at http://nces.ed.gov/programs/digest/d08/tables/dt08_026.asp?referrer=list.

Staley, O. "Stanford University Fires 49 Employees as Units Cut Budgets," 2009. Accessed December 20, 2009, at http://www.bloomberg.com/apps/news?pid=20601103&sid=a7e0D7wjp1Uc.

Reflection Questions

1. What are the sources of revenue for your institution and what is their distribution?

2. What is in-state tuition at your institution? Out-of-state? What is the approval process for setting tuition?

3. What are the fees charged to students at your institution? Which are mandatory? Are there restrictions associated with the use of the revenue from the mandatory fees?

4. What is the trend line for revenues and expenditures over the past three to five years?

5. Will these trends be likely to continue, and what are the implications for institutional planning?

6. Does your unit have access to any restricted funds? If so, for what purpose(s)?

7. How have contemporary economic conditions affected public sensitivity to either revenues or expenses at your institution?

8. Have you appropriately accounted for expense items and minimized expenses charged to the miscellaneous line so as to help accurately reflect the cost of your unit's operation?

3

Understanding Budgets

Chapter Two described the two primary elements of any budget—revenue and expenses. This chapter focuses on the budget as a whole by addressing the purposes of a budget, types of budgets, means of organizing and expressing a budget, and common budget models. The chapter also includes a discussion of decision-making processes related to budgets. The chapter concludes with reflection questions that encourage summarization, synthesis, and application of the material presented.

The term *budget* is used throughout this volume to refer to both the budget for the entire institution and the budget for a specific individual administrative or academic unit. Although the discussion in this chapter tends to focus at the institutional level, the purposes, types, and models are (and by reason of sound accounting practice ought to be) similar at all levels of a given organization.

Purposes of a Budget

Dropkin, Halpin, and LaTouche (2007, p. 3) observe, "A budget is a plan for getting and spending money to reach specific goals by a specific time." Maddox (1999) is more expansive in identifying five distinct purposes for the budget in not-for-profit organizations: putting business strategy into operation, allocating resources, providing incentives, giving control, and providing a means of communication to internal and external audiences. Although not all higher education institutions are organized as not-for-profit entities, the framework of five purposes serves to organize the discussion in this section.

Putting Business Strategy into Operation

Mayhew (1979) offers the simple but eloquent observation that "budgets are really a statement of educational purpose phrased in fiscal terms" (p. 54). The budget is one means, and arguably one of the most important means, through which an institution enacts its mission, vision, and strategic priorities as articulated in its strategic plan.

Some portion of the budget must account for the routine daily operating costs of the institution. Utilities such as heat, electricity, and water are examples of such costs. Though there is some small degree of flexibility associated with these expenses, they largely represent the relatively fixed costs associated with simply opening the doors or web portals every day. These fundamental costs are fairly stable, with adjustments made annually for inflation or other market forces.

There is a greater degree of flexibility or discretion with the balance of the budget, and it is the choices made with regard to this portion that serve as both blueprint and broadcast mechanisms for what is important at an institution. A land-grant regional university that prides itself in being student-centered and with a mission focused on access and affordability ought to have a budget that reflects that value and mission. Its budget ought to emphasize low tuition and fees, a commitment to financial aid, and strong support systems for students. The aspirations of a private research institution to increase its national profile and reputation are likely to be reflected in a budget with resources available to compete for premier faculty, provide support for such faculty, and offer support for highly qualified doctoral students, along with an investment in a strong public relations office (to support efforts through institutional relations to promote the accomplishments and qualities of the university). Tribally controlled colleges have developed unique roles in supporting the people of the tribe and maintaining tribal culture. Therefore, one would expect budgets for tribal colleges to emphasize funding for history and language preservation programs, support for child care, and ceremonies for students, family, and tribal members.

Variations in budgets are driven by more than mission, vision, and values. Institutions with significant facilities should have correspondingly significant budget lines for ongoing maintenance, as well as strong reserves available to respond to the inevitable challenges of maintenance and upkeep of aging facilities. Universities with large athletic programs may well have more substantial investments in equipment related to event management, security, and groundskeeping. In addition, such institutions may also demonstrate heightened expectations for revenue from ticket sales, advertising, or licensing agreements.

Most, but not all, higher education institutions are chartered as not-for-profit corporations. Any excess of revenues over expenditures at the end of a fiscal year are usually reinvested in pursuit of institutional goals or held in reserve for future purposes. Proprietary institutions are organized as for-profit ventures, and any excess over expenditures at the end of the fiscal year may either be reinvested in the enterprise or distributed to owners as a return on their investment.

Allocating Resources

The reality of higher education budgeting is that there are typically far more ideas for programs and services to advance the institutional mission than there are dollars to fund such ideas. Put another way, wants and needs often seem limitless whereas resources are always finite. Budgeting is the process during which an institution distinguishes between wants and needs and prioritizes needs with regard to immediacy and impact. The result of the budgeting process is the allocation of resources to the most pressing needs and, when possible and prudent, to some less pressing needs and other opportunities.

Needs are programs or services essential to performing core functions, meeting mandated requirements, or fulfilling critical expectations. An elite liberal arts institution might see offering the classic languages Greek and Latin as a need essential to their core mission whereas a similarly sized rural public baccalaureate institution might not. The latter might see courses in agriculture management or veterinary sciences as essential but the former is less likely to reach a similar conclusion. By contrast, *wants* are desirable but nonessential programs or services, including opportunities to pursue new initiatives. A nonresidential community college with a large population of adult learners might be very desirous of expanding its counseling resources, but the press for essential services in career counseling and support for students preparing to transfer in pursuit of continued education may be deemed closer to the institution's core function.

It is important to note that the allocation of resources is not limited to the allocation of new funds or the reallocation of existing funds. Changes in policy or practice may also result in freeing up other resources, such as space or human capital, that in turn allow a need or want to be fully or partially addressed without additional funds being allocated to the effort. For example, an institution that requires all first-year students to take "College Composition" and finds itself facing an unanticipated late surge in freshman enrollments might work with faculty in the English department to explore making slight increases in class sizes during peak hours or with advisors to point students toward open sections at off-peak times in an effort to meet some or all of the additional demand without increasing the budget allocation.

Providing Incentives

How an institution handles budget account balances at the end of a fiscal year can serve as either disincentive or incentive for prudent fiscal management. The practice of absorbing excess balances in unit budgets into the central budget at the close of the fiscal year can lead to rational, albeit wasteful, decisions as the fiscal year comes to a close. Units may choose to order bulk quantities of supplies and store them (thus tying up funds and space) or to purchase the latest version of software when the current version serves well (thereby wasting funds and time as staff members have to load the software, receive training, and deal with document conversion and exchange issues). Such decisions are not only less than optimal with regard to resource utilization, they can also make it more difficult to discern from budget statements the true costs of operation for a given year as they overstate expenses in the surplus year and result in understatement of expenses for the subsequent year. Some institutions that practice the absorption of excess funds attempt to control end-of-year wasteful spending through putting additional controls into place as the fiscal year comes to a close, but these practices place an additional burden on those involved in budget oversight and can serve to exacerbate frustrations at the unit level regarding the degree of central control over unit operations and budget.

An alternative approach is for an institution to allow all or some portion of excess funds to remain at the unit level at the end of the fiscal year. This approach provides an incentive for careful budget management. The unit's portion of excess funds can be transferred to a reserve account controlled by the unit where large balances can accrue over time to support major equipment purchases or investments in new initiatives. Alternatively, the excess funds can be allowed to roll over in the operating budget to allow for additional expenditures in the subsequent budget year. Although it may be desirable to provide incentives through the practice of allowing a unit to retain some portion of excess funds, it is important that such an approach not lead to overly conservative management, which impedes unit performance (for example, underinvestment in professional development or updating of printed materials). Appropriate budget adjustments should be considered for units that year after year demonstrate hefty surpluses, as the additional institutional dollars might be better allocated elsewhere.

Giving Control

One of the most singularly simple but important purposes of a budget is to provide a framework for fiscal control. That control can be understood as ranging along a continuum from highly centralized to highly decentralized. At its most extreme, a highly centralized model of budgetary control would require approval at some central point of all unit decisions regarding revenue or expenses; an equally highly decentralized model would be absent such institutional controls with full decision authority in budgetary matters resting at the unit level. Centralized decision making provides maximum control and is more likely to assure congruence between budgetary decisions and institutional priorities. It is also costly and cumbersome, as well as likely to underutilize the talents and inhibit the professional development of unit managers. A decentralized approach is more facile and allows for decision making close to the point of service or program. It requires substantial training to assure that unit managers are fully aware of budget policies and practices. However, the further the decision is from the senior administrative level the more risk there is that decisions will drift from institutional priorities.

The budgetary control model of most institutions lies somewhere along the continuum between highly centralized and highly decentralized. Typically these hybrid models provide for unit control of budgetary matters up to a set dollar limit, with decisions above that limit requiring increased levels of authority for approval. Central intervention into unit budgets is limited to larger approvals, as well as inquiries when it appears that a unit budget appears headed toward a deficit.

Providing Means of Communication

A final purpose of the budget is as a tool for communication with a variety of constituencies. The choices made with regard to budget allocations can speak volumes about what is really important for the institution. The budget reflects which programs and services receive attention in the financial decision-making process and which do not. An institution that asserts in its mission statement that it values diversity, multiculturalism, and internationalization ought to have a budget that conveys programs and services supporting those espoused values. In times of resource scarcity for those institutions, programs and services in the noted areas ought to be protected to the extent possible within the budget.

The budgets of public institutions are most often a matter of public record and generally open for inspection, including by the student media and others wishing to review institutional priorities or performance. Private institutions are not required to open their budgets to the public, but the broad outline of their budgets (like those of public institutions) may be required to be filed with state or federal agencies that in turn are required to make the information public.

The budget is a means through which institutions both public and private communicate their priorities to governing boards. Governing boards have fiduciary responsibility for oversight of institutional budget performance. This includes assuring responsible budgeting, as well as congruence between mission and commitments and institutional revenues and expenses. At some universities, the governing board as a whole reviews the institutional budget, but it is more commonly the case that such reviews are the purview of the board's finance and executive committees, whose recommendations are then reviewed and approved by the full board. Public institutions also use the budget to communicate those priorities to state legislatures and state oversight agencies.

Both public and private institutions also make their budgets available to individual donors, foundations, and other private and not-for-profit funders of higher education programs and services. In doing so, the institutions convey to potential donors how their requests for support align with current institutional priorities and how the additional funding would be put to use to advance those priorities.

Because most institutions of higher education are organized as not-for-profit entities, demonstrating accountability (as opposed to profitability) is one of the primary accounting goals for their budgets. It is for this reason that colleges and universities typically employ fund accounting as a system for organizing and reporting budgets. Using fund accounting, institutions establish specific revenue and expenditure accounts for designated purposes. All activity in those accounts must be in accord with the designated purposes.

Types of Budgets

Just as there are several common purposes of budgets, there are several common types of budgets. This section describes four common types of budgets: operating, capital, auxiliary, and special funds.

Operating Budgets

When many in higher education refer to "the budget" they are often referring to the operating budget. Meisinger and Dubeck (1984) describe the operating budget as including income from all sources (including both unrestricted and restricted funds), as well as all approved expenditures for a given fiscal year, and Woodard and von Destinon (2000) refer to the operating budget as the core budget for the institution. Cash budgets, which monitor cash flow into and out of the institution, are sometimes subsumed within the operating budget.

Reserve funds are typically included in the operating budgets of an institution, and transfers from current year operating accounts to reserve accounts are budgeted as part of prudent fiscal management. Such transfers may be mandatory as part of an ongoing policy of maintaining reserves, or they may be nonmandatory one-time transfers based on unanticipated end-of-year surpluses. Balances in reserve accounts usually roll from fiscal year to fiscal year rather than being swept clean. Examples of the ways in which reserve funds are used include funding small-to-medium renovation projects, underwriting bonds, or addressing unanticipated expenses or revenue shortfalls.

Institutional policies and procedures help shape operating budgets at all levels of the institution. For example, even if a unit is able to augment allocated funds with revenues from other sources, it must still adhere to the centrally approved range for annual salary increases in order to help assure equity across the institution.

Defining the fiscal year is another example of central authority affecting operating budgets at all levels of the institution. The definition of the fiscal year may be a decision made purely based on factors internal to the organization such as the start of the academic year at a private religiously affiliated institution, or it may primarily be a factor of functions external to the institution such as systemwide or state-based timelines for institutions that are part of state systems. One common fiscal year is September 1 through August 31, which allows for revenues and expenses associated with the summer term to be included in a single year. Another common fiscal year is July 1 through June 30. This model is frequently found at institutions with fall terms beginning in August or at public institutions aligning themselves with state fiscal years. It is relatively rare in higher education to encounter institutions making use of a fiscal year beginning January 1 and ending December 31, a model that is fairly common in the business, industry, and service sectors of the economy.

Budget managers and staff in a variety of other roles are more likely to be familiar with the operating budget of their unit and perhaps even of their institution than they are some of the other budget types. It can be helpful, however, to have a more robust understanding of the full set of budgets in play at the institution and the relationship of the other budget types to the operating budget.

Capital Budgets

Whereas an operating budget expresses revenues and expenses for a given fiscal year, a capital budget reflects revenues and expenses associated with large multiyear capital projects. These projects typically include new building construction, major building renovation, laboratory or classroom upgrades, or ongoing planned or emergency maintenance for major building systems such as roofs, plumbing, tuck-pointing, window replacement, or electrical systems. Institutions may also include the replacement of fleet vehicles or major expansions of technology such as the addition of campuswide wireless access in capital budgets.

Not all capital projects are major ones. Smaller capital projects, such as computer replacement or minor office refurbishing, are typically handled through the operating budget. Auxiliary enterprises (see below) typically do not have access to institutional capital budgets. Both capital and auxiliary budgets are discussed in greater detail in Chapter Five.

Auxiliary Budgets

In its purest form, an auxiliary enterprise in higher education is a unit that is fully self-supporting, meaning that it receives no support from the institution's operating funds. Chapter Five provides a complete discussion of budgeting as it relates to auxiliary enterprises, but it is important to note here that as a practical matter "auxiliary" comes in many flavors. Some units are indeed pure auxiliaries. Campus housing and food service operations are a common example. Other units, however, receive some partial support while still being expected to generate the bulk of their resources from outside the operating budget. Health care clinics and day care centers are often examples of this more blended model of an auxiliary enterprise.

Most colleges and universities are operated as tax-exempt entities, meaning they are not expected to pay taxes on the revenues they derive from activities related to their mission. That is not to say, however, that revenues earned for activities unrelated to the institutional mission are exempt from taxation. Indeed, colleges and universities are expected to report and pay taxes on their unrelated business income. There is growing scrutiny by policymakers of the extent to which higher education institutions are in fact living up to that expectation, and auxiliary enterprises are particularly vulnerable to that scrutiny.

Special Funds Budgets

Special funds budgets are established for designated programs or services and "indicate resources and expenses for such activities" (Goldstein, 2005). One common reason for establishing budgets specifically for such a program or service is the person or entity making the funds available has restricted the resources for that specific purpose. As an example, a special funds budget might be created for the purposes of tracking revenues and expenditures related to a gift-funded endowment for scholarships. The corpus of the endowment and interest earned on the investment of the endowment funds would be listed as revenues; the draw down of earned interest and expenses associated with the management of the endowment would be reflected as expenses. Another common example of the use of a special funds budget is grant-funded student support services such as any of the TRIO programs. Here the revenue is the grant funding, and the expenses are those directly associated with the operation of the federally funded TRIO program, as well as the *indirect costs* paid to the host institution (a term defined in Chapter Two).

Organizing and Expressing Budgets

There are two common ways of organizing and expressing budgets in higher education—functionally or naturally. Functional reporting organizes items by purpose; natural reporting organizes items by broad type (Goldstein, 2005). Common functional purposes in higher education include instruction, research, service, academic support (including libraries), student services, institutional support, facilities operation and maintenance, scholarships and fellowships, auxiliary operations, and transfers (both mandatory and nonmandatory). As noted earlier, some institutions may also have functional categories for hospital revenues and expenses.

Functional expression of revenue and expenses is particularly useful at levels of broad institutional analysis (see Table 3.1). Natural expression is arguably more practical at the unit level (see Table 3.2). A matrix organized functionally and naturally can be a particularly powerful tool in budget management (Goldstein, 2005).

It is also important in understanding a budget to recognize whether it was developed by using cash or accrual accounting. The cash system books revenue at the time it is actually received and expenses at the time they are actually disbursed. Accrual accounting recognizes revenue at the time it is earned and expenses at the time that the commitments are made.

Table 3.1.   Functional Expression of Revenues for Unit in Alpha University Hospital

Revenue Source	Budgeted	Current Period	Year to Date	Net YTD to Budgeted
Clinical	1,000,000	123,000	742,500	257,500
Sponsored research	350,000	0	175,000	175,000
Department research	0	0	0	0
Instruction	115,000	0	57,500	57,500
Administration	20,000	3,700	20,300	-300
Other	5,500	600	4,360	1,140
Total	1,490,500	127,300	999,660	490,840

Table 3.2. Natural Expression of Expenses for Administrative Unit and Academic Unit in Alpha University

Expense Type	Budgeted	Current Period	Year to Date	Net YTD to Budgeted
Salaries and Wages				
Administrative	120,000	10,000	50,000	70,000
Clerical	24,000	2,000	10,000	14,000
Student	3,600	400	2,000	1,600
S & W total	147,600	12,400	62,000	85,600
Fringe benefits	57,600	4,800	24,000	33,600
Supplies and Expenses				
Office supplies	5,100	700	2,900	2,200
Printing	2,150	0	0	2,150
Telecommunication	1,200	100	500	700
Travel	1,000	175	380	620
Minor equipment	450	450	450	0
Miscellaneous	250	25	84	166
S & E total	10,150	1,450	4,314	5,836
Unit total	215,350	18,650	90,314	125,036

Common Budget Models

The previous sections have described a variety of purposes for budgets, budget types, and means to organize and express a budget. This section discusses a number of common models for budgeting. Although this section describes the models in their pure form, rarely is it the case that a budget model is adopted and implemented in that pure form. The section closes with a discussion of the adoption and implementation of hybrid variations of budget models and a table that provides a quick reference listing the models discussed in this chapter and their strengths and limitations.

All-Funds Budgeting

The all-funds approach to budgeting emphasizes a holistic goals-oriented perspective in budget planning. This model takes into account all sources of revenue and expense as opposed to considering operating, capital, auxiliary, and special funds budgets in isolation.

Proponents argue that all-fund budgeting facilitates the monitoring of resource allocation in pursuit of institutional goals. Hence, it holds particular appeal for some in times of relative financial scarcity when institutions have a heightened sense that every financial decision is critical.

The value of the all-funds budget model is diminished at institutional levels with less budget complexity. In addition, effective implementation of an all-funds model requires a robust accounting management system that can be expensive to implement and maintain in terms of both capital expenditure and human capital.

Formula Budgeting

Formula budgeting relies on the use of specified criteria in allocating resources. Common examples of the criteria include total enrollment, enrollment growth in specific target populations, retention, graduation rates, grant-funded research, full-time employee equivalency, and gross square footage of facilities.

The vast majority of Alpha University's students are full-time, though many take just enough courses to be qualified as full-time given their need to also work while in school. Alpha University students are fairly successful in persisting to graduate. Table 3.3 illustrates the impact of various proposed state funding formulas on Alpha University's budget.

The illustration in Table 3.3 is simplistic in that it is premised on the state funding formula being calculated on one variable. The reality of state formulas is that they incorporate a variety of variables (McKeown-Moak, 2006). No one formula is inherently

Table 3.3.   Impact of Various Funding Formulas on Alpha University

Type of Formula	Rate Provided	AU Data	Funds for AU
Enrollment by headcount	$1,500 per FTE undergraduate	9,000 FTE undergraduates	$13,500,000 for undergraduate FTE
	$2,000 per FTE graduate	2,250 FTE graduates	$4,500,000 for graduate FTE $18,000,000 total
Enrollment by credit hour	$62 per undergraduate credit hour	216,000 undergraduate credit hours	$13,339,200 for undergraduate hours
	$84 per graduate credit hour	36,000 graduate credit hours	$3,024,000 for graduate hours $16,363,200 total
Degree completion	$8,000 per undergraduate $13,000 per graduate	1,800 undergraduate degrees 340 graduate degrees	$14,400,000 for undergraduates $4,420,000 for graduates $18,820,000 total

FTE = Full-time equivalent

better than any other, but the impact of formulas on institutional budgets can vary widely. It is incumbent on budget managers at institutions where funding is derived based on a formula to be aware of exactly how the formula is constructed and about any discussion regarding potential changes to the formula.

It is self-evident that in a formula budgeting model the development of the formula is a critically important process. Brinkman (1984) notes the process of defining the funding formula blends technological considerations with political purposes. He offers several recommendations to help assure that formulas are developed appropriately. Among the recommendations are being sure to include only quantifiable measures, assuring comparisons are to similar institutions, and giving consideration to the varying missions and resulting needs of institutions.

Formula budgeting is most commonly employed in public higher education in the determination of state allocations to institutions or to institutional systems. One study found that approximately two-thirds of the state systems of higher education in the United States make use of formula funding at some point in their budgeting process (McKeown-Moak, 2006). Some states use a combination of formula funding (overseen by the higher education agency within the state) and extensive legislative review of requests for new programs. The latter approach permits institutions to bring new projects and programs to the attention of the legislature without jeopardizing the basic funding base of the institution.

Proponents point to the model's transparency, efficiency of operation, and strength in linking state priorities for higher education to resource allocation. Critics argue that the formulas tend to reinforce or further privilege the larger and more selective institutions while undermining the efforts of smaller and open access institutions, as well as those that emphasize the liberal arts over preprofessional or technological fields. They further argue that the formulas are vulnerable to manipulation for political purposes.

One inherent quality of formula budgeting is that it is retrospective in nature. The data upon which the formula relies reflect experiences that have already taken place. It has been the experience of some institutions that legislatures have been slow to adjust formulas or make special appropriations in the face of suddenly changing environmental or market forces or when presented with emerging opportunities. It has also been the experience in some states that at times of fiscal stress the actual disbursement of resources has been inconsistent with the formula in place.

Incremental Budgeting

Incremental budgeting features establishing across-the-board percentage changes in expenditures for the coming budget year over the current year's budget based on assumptions regarding revenues. Incremental budgeting is fairly common in one form or another across higher education. Both the Consumer Price Index and the Higher Education Consumer Price Index are resources frequently employed to inform the size of the incremental increases made available.

Two assumptions inform incremental budgeting. The first is that the current budget is sufficient and operating efficiently to meet the priorities of the institution. Second, it is assumed that the institution's needs, wants, and opportunities (and therefore correspondingly its revenues and expenditures) are relatively stable from year to year.

In incremental budgeting's most simple form, budget managers across the institution are told to plan for X% increase in salaries and Y% in supplies and other expenses. It is not uncommon, however, for the level of specificity to occur by line item, with budget managers being informed that they should plan on X% increase in salaries; Y% increase in supplies, small equipment, and purchases; no increase for travel or professional development, et cetera. Typically the specified percentages are applied consistently throughout a particular division, but the application may vary across the institution. For example, staff salaries might be held flat while faculty salaries might increase by 1%.

Advocates of incremental budgeting point out that the model provides equal treatment for units across the institution and reduces conflict or competition that can sometimes surround matters of budget. They further observe that incremental budgeting is easy to implement and scalable across a variety of institutional models and situational contexts.

Critics point to several weaknesses in the incremental budgeting model. Whereas the critics of formula budgeting point out the potential for inequities in that model based on values embedded in the formula, critics of incremental budgeting point to the inevitable inequities in incremental budgeting that result from simple mathematics. As Maddox (1999) observes, "A unit that has a generous budget will only get better off relative to other units—its 'extra' budget grows on that budget excess, whereas another unit treads water as essential funding is increased just (or not) enough to keep pace with cost increases" (p. 16). Reliance on the current year's budget as the base for next year's budget without regard to reference to actual levels of expenditures can serve to obscure and perpetuate poor resource allocation and weak budget management, and offering poorly or modestly performing units the same increase in available resources as less dynamic or productive units is a disincentive for performance. Finally, incremental budgeting may fail to respond to changes in institutional priorities, market forces, or emerging opportunities.

Initiative-Based Budgeting

Initiative-based budgeting typically requires that all budgetary units return an identified portion of their base budgets (typically the previous year's budget adjusted for assumptions regarding increases in operating costs) to central control for the purposes of providing a pool of resources for new initiatives. These contributions may represent one-time adjustments to the unit budget, or they may be required to be recurring (or ongoing) adjustments. Units can then apply to the pool of resources that has been created to fund new initiatives that respond to identified institutional priorities. Like all-funds budgeting, the initiative-based model holds particular appeal at times of relative scarcity of new resources. Indiana University's Degrees of Excellence Initiative is one example of a systemwide initiative-based budgeting model in action (Indiana University, 2009).

It is important in implementing initiative-based funding to assure that proposals for new initiatives are not simply old stuff wrapped in new cloth. Similarly, it is critically important to assure that proposals for new initiatives are required to include specific outcomes and plans for measurement of progress toward those outcomes. Failing either of these, not only will it be less likely that institutional priorities will be fully realized, but also units may be frustrated that their sacrifices have been fruitless.

There are several strengths typically associated with initiative-based budgeting. First, units are required to reexamine their practices, programs, and performance in order to determine the ways in which they can meet the required contribution. This promotes operational efficiency. Second, through requesting modest sacrifices from across a broad spectrum of units the institution can amass a pool of sufficient size to offer the promise of a meaningful impact. Third, the process of inviting units to prepare and submit applications for the funding of initiatives encourages focus on institutional priorities and stimulates creativity in units whether or not they actually receive special funding. Finally, the act of sacrifice and redistribution can be used to demonstrate to a variety of constituencies that an institution has done what it can and is deserving of additional support.

The criticisms of initiative-based budgeting are similar in some ways to those associated with formula budgeting. The values embedded in the established institutional priorities and in the process of application and review for special funds may inherently disadvantage some units. Further, units such as facilities management or groundskeeping that provide critical core services may be expected to make a budgetary contribution but unable to articulate a new initiative in support of institutional priorities. Finally, it may be the case that some units are already minimally resourced and any sacrifice on their part would have a disproportionate impact on their programs or services.

Performance-Based Budgeting

The central feature of performance-based budgeting is that the allocation of resources is premised in no small part on attainment of specified performance measures. For example, if the business college at our fictional Alpha University is able to attract

X students to its new executive management program, then the college will be able to return the usual Y percentage of tuition revenue available to units based on the number of their majors plus an incentive of an additional Z percentage. The chairperson of biology at Alpha is also encouraging his colleagues in the department to work diligently to lower the WDF rate (those students who withdraw or earn a letter grade of "D" or "F") from 30% to 25% based on an established performance incentive that will provide funding for five new graduate assistantships and a new faculty line if the department can meet and hold that goal for three consecutive years.

Though less widely used than its cousin formula budgeting, the performance-based model has been adopted by public higher education in a number of states (McKeown-Moats, 2006) and Shin and Milton (2004) also report the implementation of performance-based budgeting in higher education systems in several countries around the world. Little information is available on the implementation of the model in private education in the United States, but the University of Cincinnati (Stripling, 2008) and Nova Southeastern University (Heron and Corbyons, 2006) are two examples of private institutions having adopted performance-based budgeting.

The strengths and weaknesses of performance-based budgeting are similar to those for formula budgeting. It is worth noting that, as is the case with formula budgeting, at public institutions appropriations often take the form of some base funding level with an additional increment being made available based on formula or performance factors.

Planning, Programming, and Budgeting Systems

Planning, programming, and budgeting systems (PPBS) is a fairly complex model for budgeting. The model is premised on tightly integrating strategic planning, budgeting, and assessment; budget decisions are a function of identifying challenges and opportunities through environmental scanning, weighing the risk-reward ratios for various alternative paths to address the identified challenges and opportunities, allocating resources in accordance with the analysis, and carefully and continuously monitoring performance and environment over a multiyear period.

PPBS was an extremely attractive budget model in its purest form, and PPBS budgeting was a popular topic of discussion in the late 1980s and 1990s, but the adoption of PPBS in higher education was limited and short lived (Woodard and von Destinon, 2000). As Birnbaum (2000) points out, management constructs quickly become management fads in higher education as a result of unique characteristics of the field. PPBS is time consuming, requires precision in articulating the desired outcomes and quantifying the potential risks and rewards, and assumes at least some period of relative stability of environment and goals. These requirements are anathema to many in higher education.

Responsibility Center Budgeting

Responsibility center budgeting locates responsibility for unit budget performance at the local level. Units are seen as either revenue centers or cost centers. Revenue centers are those units with the capacity to generate the revenues necessary to cover their expenses. In addition, these units are taxed to cover their share of central institutional services and to support the operation of cost centers. Cost centers are units that provide programs and services that do not allow for the generation of sufficient revenue to cover operating expenses. Responsibility center budgeting is also sometimes referred to as incentive-based budgeting or value-based budgeting (Hearn, Lewis, Kallsen, Holdsworth, and Jones, 2006).

Revenue centers that exceed goals with respect to budget performance are permitted to retain all or most of the excess of revenues over expenses for the following fiscal year. Cost centers may also exceed budgetary goals, but it is likely that all or most of the excesses in those units would revert to central control as opposed to carrying over in the unit. Should either a revenue or cost center underperform with regard to budget goals, the unit is responsible for addressing the shortfall through increased revenues or decreased expenses in the subsequent fiscal year.

Hearn, Lewis, Kallsen, Holdsworth, and Jones (2006) offer a thorough, insightful, and relatively rare case study of the implementation of responsibility center budgeting in higher education. Their work focuses on the experiences of the University of Minnesota in the late 1990s. Although they found that less than a quarter of the budget was directed through responsibility center budgeting, they observed that the impact of the implementation was not necessarily limited as a result of the scope of the budget affected.

Responsibility center budgeting substantially shifts budget responsibility to the unit level, a shift that may lead to increased performance and more facile responses to quickly evolving challenges and opportunities. The model encourages both entrepreneurship and innovation while providing an incentive for strong budget management.

Among the criticisms of responsibility center budgeting is that it can lead to a stratification of units within an institution ranging along a continuum from the least of the cost centers to the greatest of the revenue centers. The stratification can in turn lead to increased competition and divisiveness. Through encouraging entrepreneurship the model may also lure units to act in ways not tightly linked to institutional priorities in the pursuit of financial benefit. In addition, those who are concerned with academic capitalism (Slaughter and Leslie, 1997; Slaughter and Rhoades, 2009) may see responsibility center budgeting as technology that advances that phenomenon.

Zero-Based Budgeting

Zero-based budgeting rests on one simple proposition: each item in the budget must be justified at the time the budget is developed. There are no assumptions regarding the continuation of any program or service. Zero-based budgeting assures active monitoring of the link between institutional activities and institutional goals, with resource allocation resting on articulation of the linkage and evidence of performance.

Like PPBS, zero-based budgeting works wonderfully in theory but is nearly impossible to implement in its purest form at the practical level. The justification of each and every budget item would be an incredibly laborious process. If expenses for electrical services provided by the only local utility to a small rural private institution for electrical services have averaged around $250,000 per year for the past three years and there are not any new buildings coming online and the market for electric service appears fairly stable, how much time and labor ought to be spent justifying whether or not to pay to have the lights in working order? In addition, zero-based budgeting can have the unintended consequence of increasing anxiety regarding where programs, services, or staff positions will be funded in the coming year and provide a disincentive to commit deeply to pursuing an initiative that may or may not be funded in the future.

Zero-based budgeting is a model rarely employed in its purest form in higher education. Like most of the models discussed in this section, it is far more common to see some hybrid form of the zero-based budgeting in use.

Hybrids Are Hot

Woodard and von Destinon (2000) observe that "no one budgeting model is sufficient to meet the changing financial landscape and shifting needs of higher education" (p. 336). Hybrid models of budgeting are far and away the common mode of budgeting in higher education. An institution may use incremental budgeting to distribute new dollars across the institution but allow budget managers the flexibility within certain broad constraints (as an example, not allowing salary dollars to be used for supplies or vice versa) to redistribute those new dollars in ways the unit sees as most suitable to its needs and wants. At a time of political

Table 3.4. Strengths and Limitations of Budget Models

Budget Model	Highlights	Strengths	Limitations
All-funds	Emphasizes a holistic goals-oriented perspective Takes into account all sources of revenue and expense	Facilitates the monitoring of resource allocation in pursuit of institutional goals	Effective implementation of an all-funds model Requires a robust accounting management system
Formula	Relies on the use of specified criteria in allocating resources Development of the formula is critically important Retrospective in nature Most commonly employed in public higher education	Transparency Efficiency of operation Strength in linking state priorities for higher education to resource allocation	Tends to further privilege the larger and more selective institutions Vulnerable to manipulation for political purposes
Incremental	Establishes across-the-board percentage changes in expenditures over current budget based on assumptions regarding revenues for coming year Fairly common across higher education	Provides equal treatment for units Reduces conflict or competition Easy to implement Scalable across a variety of institutions and contexts	Inequities as the rich get richer Reliance on current budget can serve to obscure poor allocation and weak management May fail to respond to changes in institutional priorities, market forces, or emerging opportunities

Initiative-based	Requires units return portion of their budgets for the purposes of funding new initiatives May be one-time or recurring adjustments Units apply to the pool to support new initiatives	Units are required to reexamine practices, programs, and performance Can amass a substantial pool for new projects Encourages focus on institutional priorities Stimulates creativity Sacrifice and redistribution demonstrate to constituencies that institution is frugal and deserving	Values embedded in priorities and process may disadvantage some units Some core service units are expected to contribute without opportunity to create new initiatives Disproportionate impact of contributions on units with scarce resources
Performance-based	Allocation of resources premised on attainment of performance measures	Transparency Strength in linking state priorities for higher education to resource allocation	Values embedded in priorities and process may disadvantage some units Vulnerable to manipulation for political purposes
Planning, programming, and budgeting systems	Premised on tightly integrating strategic planning, budgeting, and assessment Decisions a function of identified challenges and opportunities, weighing risk-reward ratios, and monitoring performance	Tightly links budget to planning Responsive to emerging challenges and opportunities	Time consuming Requires precision regarding desired outcomes and quantifying the potential risks and rewards Assumes some period of stability

(Continued)

Table 3.4. (Continued)

Budget Model	Highlights	Strengths	Limitations
Responsibility center	Locates responsibility for unit budget performance at the local level Units are seen as revenue centers or cost centers Units are allowed to retain some portion of end-of-year budget surplus	May lead to increased performance and facile responses Encourages both entrepreneurship and innovation Provides an incentive for strong budget management	Can lead to a stratification of units Stratification can in turn lead to increased competition and divisiveness Entrepreneurship may result in decisions not tightly linked to institutional priorities Academic capitalism
Zero-based	Each item in the budget must be justified at the time the budget is developed Assures active monitoring of the link between institutional activities and institutional goals	Works wonderfully in theory Far more common to see some hybrid form	Incredibly laborious process Can increase anxiety May lead to disincentive to commit deeply to pursuing initiatives

sensitivity a public institution may single out new administrative positions or funding for office renovations for zero-based budgeting. A private institution might generally follow a responsibility center model but in a given year might blend that with a one-time initiative-based activity. It is fairly common in public higher education for state appropriations to be a sophisticated blend of incremental, formula, and performance-based budgeting.

Understanding the budget model employed at their institution is important to budget managers, but merely being able to recognize the model in play is not enough to help assure that they are able to perform their role effectively. They must also understand how decisions are made related to budgetary matters.

Decision Making and Budgets

Generally speaking the decision-making process for budgets at any institution may be described as either centrally controlled or decentralized. Both approaches are discussed in this section, which concludes with observations regarding hybrids.

Centralized Approach

The centralized approach locates all decisions regarding the budget at the institutional level with institutional priorities and goals driving the process. Stringent controls are typically in place to assure that the management of the budget throughout the fiscal year is congruent with the budget as approved.

Centralized decision making reduces the debate or tension surrounding budget development. It makes it easier to allocate resources, particularly when resources are more difficult to come by. Institutions that are struggling financially may use a centralized process of budget decision making in order to closely monitor and control expenditures. Centralization also lends itself to more readily responding to any necessary midyear adjustments to the budget either as a result of unforeseen challenges or emerging opportunities.

Centralized management, however, is not necessarily the most effective approach to budget decisions. Centralization may inhibit good budget management at the unit level as it offers neither autonomy nor much incentive to control costs. Morale may suffer in a centralized model as staff experience budget decisions related to their programs as services as being done to them or for them as opposed to with them. Centralized decision making can also lead to staff spending time and energy figuring ways around what they perceive as budget obstacles.

Decentralized Approach

A decentralized approach to budgetary decisions locates the activity at the unit level, thus effectively reversing the flow of information in the budgeting process. Budget requests are developed at the unit level to reflect the needs and wants of the unit. Decentralized budgeting takes advantage of the knowledge resident at the forefront of programs and services. Active involvement of budget managers and other staff at the unit level leads to increased buy-in for the budget, fosters proactive budget management, and allows the flexibility necessary to pursue budget performance incentives.

Like the centralized approach, the strengths of decentralized decision making are also its limitations. It is time consuming and may rest on a myopic perspective that is not tightly linked to broad institutional priorities. Competition and friction between units around budgetary matters is more likely in a decentralized decision-making process. Although morale may be low in the centralized model because of a lack of autonomy, morale can be hurt in a decentralized model when local authority leads to heightened expectations that go unfulfilled when the budget is finalized at the institutional level.

Hybrid Approaches

As is the case with budget models, few institutions adhere strictly to one approach or the other. It its far more common that the process of making decisions related to budgeting is blended, with some decisions being made at the administrative core while others are made at the unit level.

Central budget managers provide information to unit managers at the outset of the budget process regarding the broad outlines to be utilized in decision making. This may include general guidelines regarding some expense items such as salaries, new positions, or indirect costs charged to grant-funded projects or auxiliaries. Unit managers are then able to develop realistic budget requests that fall within the broad outlines while still reflecting local perspectives regarding needs and wants.

Conclusion

Knowledge of the elements of a budget and of the budget as a system are elemental to successful performance as a budget manager. These were addressed in Chapters Two and Three. Budget management and budgeting, however, are not activities that are locked into a single moment in time. Budgets have lives. They have a past, present, and future. They have a life cycle, and it is that cycle that is the focus of Chapter Four.

References

Birnbaum, R. *Management Fads in Higher Education: Where They Come From, What They Do, Why They Fail*. San Francisco: Jossey-Bass, 2000.

Brinkman, P. T. "Formula Budgeting: The Fourth Decade." In L. Leslie (Ed.), *Responding to New Realities in Funding*. New Directions for Institutional Research, no. 43. San Francisco: Jossey-Bass, 1984.

Dropkin, M., Halpin, J., and LaTouche, B. *The Budget-Building Book for Nonprofits: A Step-by-Step Guide for Managers and Boards* (2nd ed.). San Francisco: Jossey-Bass, 2007.

Goldstein, L. *College and University Budgeting: An Introduction for Faculty and Academic Administrators*. Washington D.C.: National Association of College and University Business Officers, 2005.

Hearn, J. C., Lewis, D. R., Kallsen, L., Holdsworth, J. M., and Jones, L. M. "Incentives for Managed Growth: A Case Study of Incentives-Based Planning and Budgeting in a Large Public Research University." *Journal of Higher Education*, 2006, 77(2), 286–316.

Heron, W. D., and Corbyons, V. C. "The Benefits of Performance-Based Budgeting." University Business, 2006. Accessed on November 14, 2009, at http://universitybusiness.ccsct.com/page.cfm?p=1270.

Indiana University. Office of University Planning, Institutional Research, and Accountability. Degrees of Excellence. Available at http://www.indiana.edu/~upira/projects/excellence/index.shtml. Accessed on November 14, 2009.

Maddox, D. C. *Budgeting for Not-for-Profit Organizations*. New York: Wiley, 1999.

Mayhew, L. B. *Surviving the Eighties: Strategies and Procedures for Solving Fiscal and Enrollment Problems*. San Francisco: Jossey-Bass, 1979.

McKeown-Moak, M. P. "Survey Results: 2006 Survey of Funding Formula Use." Paper presented at State Higher Education Executive Officers Conference in Chicago, IL, August 2006.

Meisinger, R. J., and Dubeck, I. W. *College and University Budgeting: An Introduction for Faculty and Academic Administrators*. Washington D.C.: National Association of College and University Business Officers, 1984.

Shin, J., and Milton, S. The effects of performance budgeting and funding programs on graduation rate in public four-year colleges and universities. *Education Policy Analysis Archives*, 2004, 12(22). Retrieved November 14, 2009, from http://epaa.asu.edu/epaa/v12n22/.

Slaughter, S., and Leslie, L. L. *Academic Capitalism: Politics, Policies, and the Entrepreneurial University*. Baltimore: Johns Hopkins University Press, 1997.

Slaughter, S., and Rhoades, G. *Academic Capitalism and the New Economy: Markets, States, and Higher Education*. Baltimore, MD: John Hopkins University Press, 2009.

Stripling, J. "'Free Market' for Higher Ed." *Inside Higher Ed*. November 11, 2008. Available at http://www.insidehighered.com/news/2008/11/11/cincinnati. Accessed on November 14, 2009.

Woodard, D. B. Jr., and von Destinon, M. "Budgeting and Fiscal Management." In M. J. Barr, and M. K. Desler (Eds.), *The Handbook of Student Affairs Administration* (2nd ed.). San Francisco: Jossey-Bass, 2000.

Reflection Questions

1. What are the purposes of the budget at your institution?

2. What does your institution's budget say about its priorities? In what ways is your answer similar or different with regard to your unit's budget?

3. How is the distinction made between your unit's needs and wants?

4. What has your involvement been with operating budgets? Capital budgets? Auxiliary budgets? Special funds budgets?

5. Does your institution use natural or functional accounting?

6. How do you describe the budget model used at your institution? What do you see as its strengths and limitations?

7. What budget approach is used at your institution? How do you feel it serves your unit? The institution?

4

Management of the Budget Cycle

B udget management is a never-ending task for any administrator with financial responsibilities in higher education. In fact,
administrators–budget managers who understand the cycles of budgets in higher education recognize that they are never managing
just one budget. The person with budget management responsibilities in the unit is likely to be supervising expenditures under the
current operating budget and closing or getting ready to close
the previous year's operating budget while making financial projections for the upcoming fiscal year. If new facilities are in the planning stages or under construction attention must also be given to
the capital budget (which may have timing issues different from
those of the operating budget). If the unit is involved in management of a facility then attention must also be given to building operating costs and plans for ongoing maintenance and repair.
(See Chapter Five.) Those same budget administrators may also be
asked to project budgets beyond the current and next fiscal year in
order to support the overall fiscal plan of the institution. Finally,
management of the budget (as noted in the previous chapter) is
not limited to merely projecting expenses; it also involves estimat-
ing revenues from all sources that support the budget of the unit.
Because of the complexity of the task, those with budget responsibility often feel like they are juggling several balls at the same time.

This chapter focuses on the budget cycle involved in developing and implementing the operating budget for any budgetary unit
within any institution of higher education. It focuses on the steps
involved in developing a new budget request as well as the processes
and procedures that are helpful in ongoing budget management.

It also discusses forecasting both revenue and expenses into future fiscal years. Auxiliary and capital budget development and forecasting (which are usually a special case) are covered in Chapter Five.

General Issues

There are a number of general issues that influence the development of the budget in any institution: institutional characteristics, the participants in the process, and the amount of time available to seek input on budgetary matters.

Institutional Characteristics

Institutional size and complexity influence both the budget process and who is involved in the development of the institutional budget. Goldstein indicates, for example, that "Colleges with small faculties and staffs and a strong sense of shared governance will probably have relatively open deliberations. Large institutions or those without a highly participative governance structure will more likely have a relatively closed budget process without much input from constituents. Generally speaking a more open process is desirable" (2005, p. 98).

Even in large institutions there are methods to involve more constituent groups into the budget decision-making process through avenues such as advisory committees or open forums. The culture and history, as well us the public or private nature of the institution, will, however, dictate what the acceptable methods are to develop an institutional budget.

Participation

When encouraging participation in the process, however, care should be given to the actual process of determining the representatives who will participate. A formal process to select representatives is useful as is clarity about what participation in the budget process actually means in terms of decision making and information. For example, at a large private institution undergraduate students were interested in becoming more involved in the budget process. A process was developed whereby a representative group of students was chosen by students to represent them in the budget process. They were named the Undergraduate Budget Priorities Committee. The committee annually seeks general input from the student body about needs and wants. This student committee, in turn, makes a formal presentation to the University Budget Committee on student priorities, which are then considered as part of the total budget process. Under such circumstances items that were not considered a priority by faculty and administrative staff are sometimes built into budget allocations because the concepts were carefully vetted and presented by the student committee. In addition, student concerns about not having a voice in the budget process were alleviated.

Available Time

Time is also a large factor in how inclusive a budget process can be. If, in a public institution, the budget process is delayed because of lack of action by the state legislature then involvement opportunities on the campus become more constrained. Under such circumstances the campus administration should clearly communicate the causes for delay and perhaps still provide opportunities (even in uncertain conditions) for members of the community to express their funding requests. Private institutions usually can exercise more control over the budget development timetable. However, unexpected budget shortfalls can cause any timetable to be altered. In both types of institutions those administrators with responsibility for development of the institutional budget should communicate any delays or changes as soon as they are finalized to interested members of the campus community.

The Fiscal Year Operating Budget

Each fiscal year operating budget has eight distinct phases: setting institutional and unit budget guidelines, developing the unit budget request, identifying the budget implications of that request beyond the budget fiscal year, approving the budget, monitoring budget performance, adjusting the current operating year budget, closing the fiscal year, and analyzing budget performance at the end of the fiscal year. Some of these phases occur simultaneously and some are sequential.

Figure 4.1.　A Typical Budget Unit Cycle

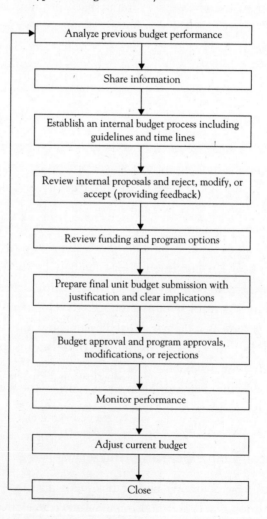

Setting Guidelines

Budget guidelines and rules are set on the institutional level and can differ markedly between public and private institutions. Public institutions need to develop institutional budget guidelines that are congruent with overall state fiscal policies whereas private institutions are under no such restrictions. At both types of institutions, additional budget guidelines may also be developed for various subunits within the college or university. For example, a dean or vice president might want to reserve part of the money allocated for raises in a central pool that could be used to provide additional salary increments for faculty and staff members who have provided extraordinary service. Such a decision is permitted in most institutions as long as the internal rules of the academic or administrative unit are consistent with institutional parameters.

Institutional Guidelines and Parameters

Institutional guidelines for budget submission are usually issued very early in the budgeting process. These guidelines are set after a great deal of study and debate within the central administration and the budget office of the institution. Setting budget parameters is not an easy task and requires the institutional financial staff to conduct an environmental scan and to analyze the past budget performance of all budgetary units in the institution. Cost overages are highlighted and instances in which projected costs did not rise as much as anticipated are noted. Understanding where prior institutional budget parameters were accurate and where they missed the "mark" is the first step in the development of new institutional budget guidelines.

Institutional guidelines also set the "outside limits" for spending. They are usually couched in "not to exceed" language. For example, "increases in travel may not exceed 2%." Separate decision rules usually govern personnel and other operating budget expenditures. Personnel budget rules usually set the limit for total budget commitments in each unit for salaries and benefits for all full-time, part-time, and student employees. Usually institutions do not permit transfer from personnel lines to other items in the budget without express permission. In addition, at some institutions (primarily in the public sector) explicit permission must be given to add permanent personnel lines to any budget request. This is a political issue since the growth in the number of positions at state supported institutions of higher education is a sensitive topic in many state legislatures. The general institutional guidelines are developed after careful study of the environment and the issues influencing the operation of the institution.

Environmental Scan

The scan of the outside environment is an essential second step in the development of institutional budget guidelines. Identification of the outside forces that will influence the budget at the institution requires a rigorous environmental scan. For example, will the cost of utilities rise in the next budget year, and if the answer is yes, what is the best prediction of how much utility costs will change? Different percentages of change will be assigned to each utility (water, electricity, gas, oil, other fuels) and will be part of the final institutional budget parameters. Questions should be asked regarding whether there are alternate sources for any utility. To illustrate, at one state institution an enterprising vice president for finance and planning saved the institution thousands of dollars in energy costs by negotiating a contract for natural gas directly from the producer rather than with a regional distributor.

Other external cost factors will also be built into the budget parameters through the environmental scan. These might include the cost of insurance, the cost of obtaining services (fire safety for example) from the local municipality, the local experience in negotiation with unions that are represented in the campus workforce, the rate of return on investments, or any changes in fees for banking services. To be an effective budget development tool, the environmental scan needs to be broad and identify as many outside forces as possible that may influence the financial health of the institution in the year to come.

Depending on the institutional size and type the environmental scan may be complex, done by an institutional office, outsourced to a private business, or done by one astute financial officer who pays attention to the influence that the outside environment has on the operations of the institution.

Past Performance

Past performance is thought by many to be an indicator of future performance when it comes to budgets. A review of past performance of all line items across the institution is usually an essential step in developing budget guidelines. Problem areas are identified. For example, when gasoline prices rose steeply the cost of transportation in individual units also rose and sometimes exceeded the budget. As the new budget guidelines are developed such past performance issues must be identified and understood. Any large variance between the planned budget and actual performance across the institution and in individual units is studied in detail and is accounted for in the development of institutional guidelines.

Planning Processes

Finally, a strong link must be established between any institutional planning processes and the new institutional budget guidelines. If, for example, a strategic institutional goal is to reduce the turnover of support staff then the institutional budget guidelines would address rates of compensation, benefits, and training for such staff. Or if a new program initiative is identified as part of the institutional strategic plan, then the budget guidelines must accommodate that new initiative at the institution. For example, if the institution has decided to adopt a program of having new students all read the same book and discuss it during new student orientation that decision has budget implications. Money must be allocated for all aspects of that program, including personnel, book purchases, discussion guides, and evaluation. Or if a new academic program in Asian-American Studies has been approved then all costs for support of the new academic program need to be built into the operating budget, including the recruitment and hiring of new faculty. In addition, a fiscal plan must be developed and approved for the ongoing budgetary support and eventual expansion of the new academic program. Or if the institution has adopted a goal to increase alumni fiscal support from 25% to a 50% participation rate over the next five years, then budget allocations must be made to support the work that would be required to achieve that goal.

It is clear that the process of developing institutional budget guidelines is based on a series of assumptions and beliefs. Budget guidelines, however they are determined, will reflect the assumptions held by planners regarding enrollment, demand for services, opportunities, and problems facing the institution. It is critical that every budget manager understand the assumptions and beliefs that drive the institutional budget guidelines. If a unit budget manager does not understand those assumptions, clarification should be sought. Sources for clarification include the central budget office or administrative superiors. It is only when the manager understands the rationale for guidelines that credible requests can be made for additional resources.

Timetables

Institutional budget instructions also include the timetable for submission of all budget documents. Once the institutional timetable is established then an administrator with budget responsibilities can establish earlier schedules for budget request submissions within the unit. Institutional timetables should never be ignored, and every effort should be made to meet the institutional deadlines. If problems arise in meeting the timetable, those issues should be discussed *as soon as possible* with the appropriate administrative office (dean, division, vice president, and so forth) to both inform them of the problem and determine whether there is any flexibility in deadlines. Ignoring deadlines or being chronically late in submission of budget materials can, in the long run, adversely affect the budget of the unit. Table 4.1 shows a typical institutional budget schedule and a unit budget schedule.

Table 4.1.   Typical Institutional and Unit Budget Schedules

Institutional Schedule	Unit Schedule
	July 31 Remind units of closing deadlines
August 31 Close the FY	August 31 Close the FY
September 1–30 13th month clean up	September 1–30 13th month clean up Begin review of last FY performance Begin aspirational conversation within unit
October–December Institutional budget guidelines developed Revenue planning assumptions developed	October–December Clear up any problems with prior FY Begin monitoring current FY Internal review of new proposals Check assumptions in proposals Update strategic plan
November–March Meet with units to review strategic plans	November–March Review strategic plan with administration Adjust strategic plan Continue to monitor current budget Internal prioritization of new proposals
December Review of last FY performance by trustee budget committee Approval of tuition, fees, and room and board rates for next FY by trustee budget committee Approval of budget parameters for next FY by trustee budget committee	

(Continued)

Table 4.1.   (Continued)

Institutional Schedule	Unit Schedule
March	March
Faculty salary plans sent to schools	Respond to faculty salary plans (if applicable)
	Continue to monitor current budget
April	April
Finalize and distribute budget allocations for next FY	Develop and share unit budget guidelines
	Finalize new program proposals
May	May
Faculty hiring plans due to provost	Finalize unit budget requests (including new program proposals), being sure to check and confirm figures
Detailed appropriated budgets for units due at budget office	
Budget summary prepared for trustees	Submit appropriated budget
Exempt and non-exempt staff salaries due at human resources	Respond to questions regarding budget requests
	Prepare and submit staff salary proposals
	Continue to monitor current budget
June	June
Budget for next FY approved by trustees	Continue to monitor current budget
July	July
Approved budget for next FY entered into financial systems	Continue to monitor current budget
	Remind unit of closing rules for current FY
August	August
Budgets for upcoming FY distributed to units	New budget allocations distributed
Closing process for current FY begins	Begin closing process
September 1	September 1
Begin new fiscal year	Begin new fiscal year

Forecasting Expense and Revenue

As part of the development of institutional guidelines, a unit budget manager will often be asked to assist the institutional budget office in forecasting outcomes for the current budget year and beyond. This is a routine part of the planning process, and unit budget managers should be prepared to share their best thinking about what the current fiscal year will eventually look like and what the future might be. Forecasting is, at best, an inexact process, so a word of caution is in order. *Revenues should be forecast as conservative figures but expenses should not!* If revenues are forecast at the highest possible level, those unit-based forecasts are often accepted and incorporated into the institutional planning process. When the forecasted revenue goal is not met then there may be negative budget consequences for the unit.

Obviously, forecasting for the end of the current fiscal year is a great deal easier than projecting revenue and expenses several years into the future. The prior budget analysis conducted by the unit budget manager (see next section) will provide valuable information. How has the unit done in the past? Have there been great variances between the budget plan and the final budget outcome? What was the cause of those variances? In addition, if the current fiscal year budget is being monitored regularly, the unit budget manager is aware of any problems that may influence the bottom line for the unit and can use that information as part of the year-end forecast.

Forecasting beyond the current fiscal year becomes more inexact. A multiple year performance should be based on past experience and performance of the unit. Further, the forecast should be closely linked to the planning process within the unit and the institution. For example, if a grant is a major part of the income for an academic department, what will happen when the period of the grant is completed? Are there other sources of funds to support the activities formerly supported by the grant? Is the department expecting the institution to pick up those costs? Will the faculty and staff supported by the grant be terminated? These are difficult questions and cannot be answered by a unit budget manager alone, but they must be answered if the multiple year forecast is to be accurate.

A multiple year forecast should be based on the data regarding past performance, information from an environmental scan, and the unique issues faced by the unit. To be helpful to institutional planners and the unit a forecast should be as realistic as possible and not raise either positive or negative expectations that are not likely to occur.

In addition, when a forecast is made the assumptions underlying that forecast must be clear. If institutional budget managers do not understand the underlying assumptions of the forecast, miscommunication can occur. It is usually helpful to develop a series of "what if" scenarios when making multiple year forecasts. Those alternative scenarios help clarify assumptions and highlight concerns faced by the institution and the unit. To illustrate, if a forecast is presented for future enrollment in a new master's level program in information technology, that forecast should explain how the projected enrollment figures were developed and any assumptions that were made regarding the payment of tuition for these additional graduate students.

Developing Unit Budget Requests

At a minimum there are ten specific steps that can help in the development of understandable and carefully developed individual unit budget requests. Some of these steps occur simultaneously and others are done in sequential order.

Analyze Previous Unit Budget Performance

Even if you are a new budget manager it is important to carefully analyze the prior year's budget performance of the unit. Did the unit end the last fiscal year with a surplus or a deficit? If so, why did that occur? Is there a pattern over the years of over- or under-expenditures or revenue shortfalls or surpluses in some line items? Can determination be made about why these occur? Use of a three-year rolling average of expenditures and revenue is one way to account for year-to-year variances.

These questions can assist in determining whether there are chronic fiscal problems or issues within the unit. Understanding clearly what happened in the past sets the stage for a frank and open discussion with colleagues in the unit as well as the central budget office. The focus of those discussions should be on jointly determining the reasons behind apparent anomalies in the previous operating budget(s) of the unit. This type of analysis prepares a budget manager to ask focused questions when developing the unit budget request for the next fiscal year so that the budget request accurately reflects the needs of the unit. Also, such a process provides valuable information to decision makers outside the unit when such justification is presented for any large changes in the departmental budget request.

Share Information

Budget development is not a secret process, although it seems that way in some collegiate environments. Information regarding the parameters established by the institution and the rationale for those budget rules should be shared widely within the agency or department preparing the budget request. Faculty and staff need to understand why certain decisions were made. Sometimes faculty and staff will disagree with the reasons for a specific institutional budget guideline or feel that their situation is unique and falls outside the stated institutional parameters. Sharing budget information can be a frustrating task for a budget manager when such attitudes surface. However, Woodard and von Destinon (2000) indicate that information sharing stimulates all members of the organization to think creatively about solutions to ongoing problems and issues associated with the budget.

Establish an Internal Unit Budget Process

The internal budget process within the unit should be clear and unambiguous. Everyone involved in the budget process should be made aware of how and when decisions will be made regarding ideas and proposals that they may bring forward. Budget requests are rarely the work of just one person within a unit. Although the ultimate responsibility for the budget submission remains with the dean, chair, or other unit head, development of a process that includes wider input helps inform decisions. Most often, a budget committee is formed within the department or unit to help prioritize the needs of the department. In smaller units, the use of a "committee of the whole" permits everyone in the department to have an opportunity to comment on needs and wants for the unit. No matter what process is chosen, it is critical that the budget of the unit reflects unit goals and objectives and is consistent with stated unit plans and priorities.

As part of the unit budget process, additional internal guidelines may be set within the unit and applied to all programs. For example, if travel support is a source of frustration, then a multiyear review of travel expenditures will assist in establishing a rationale for travel support and will influence the final distribution to that line in the proposed budget. Once a process is established it should be followed. Nothing frustrates people more than trying to play by "the rules" and then discovering exceptions have been made for other individuals or programs within the organization.

Listen

It is essential to provide an opportunity for members of the organization to be heard regarding their needs and wants both before and during the budget preparation process. Depending on the size and complexity of the unit, formal hearings or informal conversations can be held. The important task is to provide a genuine opportunity for members of the organization to express their hopes, concerns, and aspirations for the coming year(s) and to assure them that their ideas are seriously considered by the unit budget manager and other decision makers within the unit. These discussions or formal hearings should not be pro forma but should instead provide an opportunity to explore "what if" scenarios with persons responsible for program implementation. To illustrate, perhaps the head of an academic tutoring program indicates that in order for the program to succeed a new staff person must be added to the program. The process of careful listening aids in determining what will *not* occur if the new position is *not approved*. It also affords an opportunity to explore other alternatives to meet the identified need, including the use of additional graduate students, student workers, and outsourcing.

Finally, the process of having conversations and hearings regarding dreams, aspirations, wants, and needs does *not* have to wait until formal institutional budget guidelines are issued. In fact, early conversations about such aspirations may make the budget development process move forward in a much more efficient and effective manner.

Establish Internal Guidelines

The budget timetable for the unit will be much shorter and start much earlier than the institutional timeline. Communication about the internal timetable for the unit regarding creating and submitting budget materials (including proposals for new or expanded support) is critical. In addition, the budget manager should develop a unit timetable that permits review of both the short-term and long-term implications of a new and continuing budget request.

Unit budget guidelines should also detail the decision parameters regarding each line item or categories of line items in the budget. Such guidelines should easily inform those expected to develop budget proposals about the form for submission, the limits on submissions, the expectations for justification of the request, the long- and short-term implications of the request, and so forth. The guidelines need not be lengthy, but they must be clear and easy to understand. As part of the unit budget guidelines a clear invitation should be issued for those who have questions to ask them and to seek clarification of issues prior to beginning to work on budget requests. Such an approach saves both time and energy on the part of everyone involved in the budget process by avoiding redoing submission materials. Exhibit 4.1 provides a sample of unit budget guidelines.

Review Proposals

Requests for new funding or increased funding from programs or departments should be linked to the plan for the unit and the objectives of the institution. Each proposal should also outline the implications of the proposal beyond the fiscal year in question.

Exhibit 4.1.   Typical Additional Unit Budget Guidelines

1. Read the institutional guidelines very carefully. If you have questions see _____ (insert person's name) immediately.

2. The Dean/Director is reserving 0.5% of the salary increment money to provide extraordinary increments across the division. Therefore your increment dollars are _____.

3. Provide in writing your assumptions underlying the costs in your proposed budget. For example how many students will be served? What is the cost per student?

4. If you are submitting a new program proposal include the following:
   a. Who will be served?
   b. What is the cost per student?
   c. Why is this new initiative important?
   d. How does this new initiative connect to our unit strategic plan?
   e. What is the total budget for the new initiative?
   f. What revenue will support the plan? (Use our program plan budget document [attached] to answer these questions.)

What impact will the proposal have for funding in future years? The answer to that question determines the real costs to the institution.

A budget proposal should include the rationale for the request and present a clear picture of how the institution will benefit if the proposal is funded. This rationale should be stated in plain English and should not be filled with jargon. Where possible, data should be provided in support of the request. Those reading the proposal should be able to easily answer the questions such as, What will change as the result of funding this proposal? What will remain the same? How many people will be served? And how will success be measured?

In addition, if anticipated savings are part of the funding proposal, examine the proposal very carefully. Are the savings real? Off-loading a program to another agency might save money for the department shedding the program but there are no real savings for the institution. Further, a proposal to reallocate funds to other purposes through elimination of a program should be very carefully evaluated. The question of whether the program can be eliminated must be answered, for if it is politically impossible to eliminate an old program to support a new effort, then the savings are not real. Such issues must be identified and assessed early in the budget development process. The basic arithmetic of the proposal should also be carefully checked. Arithmetical errors happen all the time and should be identified and rectified prior to forwarding any budget proposal from the unit. Finally, routine inflationary cost increases should not be just accepted, even if they are consistent with the general guidelines from the institution. All budget increase requests should be reviewed and the underlying assumptions for the increase should be tested. Auxiliary enterprises provide some of the best examples of the need for such testing. For example, most institutions have seen a sharp rise in utility costs. The institutional environmental scan, as well as information from the electricity provider, identified the acceptable percentage increase for electric costs for the coming fiscal year. The easy way to build the budget for the next year is to apply the rate increase percentage to the currently budgeted line item for electricity, but that is not the most accurate approach and may present a false picture. The budget analysis discussed earlier in this chapter should provide data on what the actual cost for electricity was last year and an average cost for over the last three years. Unless a new building has been added or taken off line, that calculated figure should become the base for applying the percentage increase allowed for electricity for the new fiscal year. Other approaches could also be used, including taking the highest use year and projecting costs with an inflation factor into the current fiscal year and using that as a new base. It may mean that those calculations will result in a savings in the line item for electricity, but it also might mean that electricity costs should be budgeted at a higher level than is approved in the institutional budget guidelines. If that is the case, then the difference can either be met through reallocation or relief can be sought from the institution.

A word of caution is in order here. Before a complete budget review of a unit occurs, a decision should be made whether the process itself will be cost effective. In other words, should a budget manager spend his or her time in more productive ways? Most budget managers review only a few key line items in a given fiscal year because of time constraints unless they are operating under a zero-based budgeting model (see Chapter Three). It is essential, at this stage, that the next level of the administration (dean or vice president) be informed about the aspirations and plans of the unit. If he or she has any concerns about the new program proposal they can be addressed prior to budget submission. Those administrators with responsibility for the unit should also be involved when options are being explored to provide funding for a new initiative, for they are privy to information that would be extraordinarily helpful to those wanting to begin a new initiative (see next section).

Review Options

It is an axiom that there is never enough money to meet all requests made at the department, unit, or institutional level. When there is a shortfall between requests and income the easy answer is just to say no and move on. A strategic budget manager, however, should test the feasibility of other options. Those options might include developing a source of income to support the new program or service. Another option might be to eliminate or curtail a current program or activity in order to start a new initiative. As noted earlier, this option must be carefully examined to assure that other units within the institution will not be adversely influenced by such a decision. Dickeson's *Prioritizing Academic Programs and Services* (2010) provides a well-developed discussion on how to prioritize program initiatives.

A third approach is to carefully examine whether cost savings could be captured by changing the way business is done within the unit. To illustrate, one approach might be to change the means of communicating to students from traditional letters to e-mail. Another approach might include examining whether some full-time positions could be modified to part-time or whether twelve-month positions could be converted to academic year positions without negatively affecting services to faculty, staff, and students. Ask the members of the unit to suggest what might be done to garner savings to start a new program. Their creativity might be surprising and may help identify resources to support the new venture.

Provide Feedback

Improvement of the quality of requests and the accuracy of submitted budget documents will only occur if feedback is given to the person(s) making the budget proposal. If the proposal is not supported at the unit level then the individual(s) who submitted the proposal deserve feedback on why it was not supported. It is only through such feedback that the staff and faculty members involved can improve their work and future proposals. If the proposal cannot be fully funded but can be supported at some lower level, then information sharing is also critical. Many new programs fail because budget managers make unilateral decisions of what can be eliminated or modified in the program plan. The person(s) who made the proposal should be consulted regarding where reductions can be made in the program that will have the least negative influence on the proposed new program plan.

Prepare Final Budget Submission(s)

After all the final decisions regarding the budget request are made at the unit level (including strategies for reallocation and cost savings), it is time to prepare the final documents for the budget request. Usually there are several steps in budget submission from a unit. The budget materials need to be approved by the dean, director, or vice president. Often, if they have not been privy to the departmental discussions some new budget requests may take them by surprise. Surprising the dean or vice president at this stage of budget development should be avoided if at all possible. The earlier such administrators are included in the planning process the more effective they can be as advocates for the new initiative.

Properly prepared budget documents submitted to the central budget office in a timely fashion will receive the warranted attention. Submissions that are difficult to read, are sloppily done, or do not provide all the requested information probably will not be considered carefully or positively. Follow the institutional guidelines carefully and ask for clarification if there is uncertainty regarding the form or substance of the budget request. As part of the budget request, whether it is asked for or not, prepare a statement clarifying the implications of the new request beyond the current fiscal year.

Implications

Failure to identify the implications of the budget request to other offices or agencies across the institution is a critical mistake often made by new budget managers. For example, if a budget request for additional tutoring support is predicated on reducing support for an orientation program for new graduate students, then that should be clearly noted in the budget request. As another illustration, consider the unit that has submitted a proposal for federal funds to support community service learning opportunities for undergraduates. The original grant proposal included creation of new professional staff positions and a statement that the institution will provide matching funds for the implementation of the program. Legitimate questions that should be asked when approval is sought for the grant proposal are: What will happen when the grant expires? How will the program be institutionalized? What are the potential costs for such institutionalization?

Alternatively, the new budget request might be to support the addition of two new tenure-track faculty positions. Such a proposal requires an addition to the base budget of the requesting department, including both salary and benefits. There are also other costs that must be accounted for in the new budget request. Such hidden costs might include funding for space, equipment, supplies, and money for additional support staff. Requests are more likely to be positively considered if data clearly support the need and it is clear (from the budget proposal) that the department understands and appreciates the long-term ramifications of the request beyond salary and benefits. Exhibit 4.2 provides a series of questions that may help budget managers miss some of these pitfalls in preparing budget documents.

Exhibit 4.2.   Six Pitfalls in Preparing Budget Documents

The following pitfalls often occur in preparing budget documents:

1. Failure to understand institutional guidelines. Ask questions frequently and often and do not assume you understand.

2. Failure to check computations. Simple arithmetical errors can occur so check your submission carefully.

3. Failure to connect the new proposal to the unit and institutional strategic plan.

4. Failure to clearly state what *will* occur if the proposal is funded.

5. Failure to clearly state what *will not occur* if the proposal is not funded.

6. Failure to account for ancillary costs (staff and faculty benefits, room rentals, etc.).

Approving the Budget

The budget approval process is iterative. It is very unusual for a budget request to be submitted for approval without additional information being sought or hearings held. With financial management being only one of many responsibilities for most administrators, many give a sigh of relief when the budget materials are submitted and hope that their responsibilities are over. They are not. Most often, no matter how thorough the budget submission, there will be requests from the central budget office or the review committee for clarification of certain items. In addition, it is not unusual for a request to be returned for modifications or reductions of program scope. Everyone involved in preparing the budget request should understand that all budget requests will not and cannot be funded (consider the case of Alpha University). Lack of funding does not necessarily mean that the program or idea is without merit. It may merely mean that funding options were limited and other priorities were funded as opposed to the unit request.

Once the institutional budget is created (from unit requests as modified), it is presented to the governing board for approval. This process is not automatic and may contain surprises both positive and negative. Usually a great deal of communication occurs prior to presenting the final budget documents to the governing board. Earlier in the year the institutional parameters were discussed and agreed upon by the governing board and the institutional administration prior to campus distribution. Enrollment projections are agreed upon with the governing board, and the size of the entering class is determined. The institutional investment strategy is approved, and the spending rules regarding the income from the endowment have been approved by the governing board. In addition, the board audit committee may raise questions about the financial performance of certain units and income or deficit projections. Final budget approval by the governing board *only* occurs after a long process of information sharing and decision making by the board and its committees and the institutional administration.

Continuous Management of the Operating Budget

After the budget is approved and the fiscal year begins, the approved budget must be monitored. Monitoring the budget is a constant task even when the budget manager is preparing budget requests for the next fiscal year.

Monitoring the Budget

In an ideal world monitoring budget performance would be an easy task. Each month the expenses charged against the various accounts in the budget unit would be equal to one-twelfth of the operating budget approved for the unit. If expenditures proved to be more than one-twelfth of the budget, then the budget manager would immediately know that there was a problem. Unfortunately, the world of a budget manager is far from ideal.

Rarely are expenses equally divided from month to month, and errors may be made in both accounting and billing.

The diligent budget manager monitors budget performance each and every month by reviewing all budget reports. In order to be effective at the task, the budget manager must understand the ebb and flow of the budget and the institutional rules governing accounting and charges.

What information should the budget manager review prior to raising concern about budget performance? Any number of factors could cause a problem in the monthly budget report. For example, are salaries for faculty and staff automatically encumbered for the entire academic or fiscal year? Are those encumbrances accurate in terms of agreed upon salary and the number of months the employee should be paid? If encumbrances are used at the institution to protect personnel dollars in the budget, then personnel expenses in the early months of the fiscal year might appear to be alarmingly high but are not really a cause for concern.

Or the budget may contain an allocation for a major piece of equipment. If that is true, then the dollars to support the purchase order for that equipment may have already been encumbered even if the equipment has not yet arrived.

Finally, are there known expenses that will not be charged to the budget until much later in the fiscal year? For example, does the unit sponsor a summer research program? If so, money must be reserved within the budget to support the program. Each unit will have unique expenses and unique questions that must be asked and answered in a preliminary review of the monthly accounting statements of the unit. The questions outlined above are merely illustrative of the type of probing questions by the budget manager to determine, as soon as possible, whether there is a problem that must be addressed. Once the answers to these broad questions are clear, it is time to dig into the monthly budget report. All expense and revenue lines that are not congruent with the budget plan need to be carefully examined.

To illustrate, if the approved budget for office supplies is $10,000 for the entire fiscal year and $5,000 is charged against the office supply line in the first month budget report, questions need to be raised. It could be that the vendor billed the unit twice for the same order. Or it might be that an enterprising staff member bought supplies for the entire year because of a deep discount offered for bulk purchases. Or perhaps the cost of a new computer was charged against the office supplies line rather than the budget line for equipment purchases. A final reason was that the person responsible for ordering supplies paid absolutely no attention to the budget. Each of these reasons requires a different response by the budget manager. Billing errors can be corrected, accounting errors can be reversed, initiative on the part of the enterprising staff member can be praised, and the person ignoring the limitations of the budget must be confronted. In order to stay on top of the budget, every line item should be reviewed with a high degree of specificity.

Further, if the unit relies on multiple sources of revenue to help meet the expense budget, then review of revenue performance against revenue goals should also be routine. If it appears that revenues are falling below expectations, then a number of issues should be reviewed before any action is taken. For example, is the shortfall in revenue related to an activity occurring later in the fiscal year? Or if the revenue is from mandatory fees, is the amount credited to the unit budget congruent with enrollment figures? Addressing those questions is necessary in order to determine whether there is a genuine shortfall and whether or not corrective action should be taken.

Adjusting the Current Budget

If there is a revenue shortfall, then expenses, where possible, should be adjusted downward to cover at least part of the projected deficit. To illustrate, a freeze could be placed on ordering new equipment until the shortfall problem has been resolved.

Another strategy is to determine whether there are other sources of income that might be increased or identified to meet part of the budget need. In either case, a significant shortfall should not be ignored but highlighted and communicated to the administrative unit responsible for overseeing the department. Ignoring such problems will only compound the difficulty in addressing the issue.

Finally, if there are uncontrollable costs being faced by the unit, then these problems must also be identified and communicated. Examples of such unforeseen costs might be an increase in postal rates, or an increase in the rates for workers' compensation that was not even on the horizon when the budget was prepared or approved. These kinds of problems are issues that cannot be solved by the unit budget manager alone. They have implications for the entire institution, and decision makers and financial staff need to partner with unit budget managers in solving the problem.

When a strategy is developed to address the problem issue, adjustments may be made to the current fiscal year budget. One strategy might involve transferring money to the operating budget from an institutional reserve account. Another strategy might involve transferring money from a different line item within the unit. Institutional rules and accounting practices will influence whether or not actual adjustments are made in the official institutional budget. If the printed or on-line budget is not adjusted, then the prudent manager should document any agreement with the central budget office for the record. Such documentation will serve as a reminder of the problem and the agreed upon solution at the close of the fiscal year.

Closing

To close the budget means that no more activity may be charged against or revenue added to the budget for that fiscal year. Invoices for goods and services not paid by the time of closing may be charged against the budget of the unit in the new fiscal year. If these items are substantial there could be an adverse impact on budget performance in the next fiscal year.

In order to try to minimize some of these issues institutions have established three key dates related to the closing of the fiscal year. The first relates to the last day that new purchase orders can be processed against the current fiscal year budget. Usually, that date is three to four weeks prior to the end of the current fiscal year. This regulation reduces the number of outstanding purchase orders (invoices) at the close of the fiscal year. The second date refers to the beginning of the new fiscal year. It is the date when all budget expenses and revenues will be charged to the new fiscal year budget. This date may be prior to the actual calendar date for the fiscal year. The last date is the final closing date for the budget from the previous fiscal year.

Most often the final closing date is set one month after the calendar close of the fiscal year. Known by some as the thirteenth month, this extended closing date permits larger invoices to clear and not be charged in the new fiscal year. If an institution uses the thirteenth month strategy, then there are usually limitations on the amount and types of charges and income that may be posted during the thirteenth month period against the prior fiscal year. The thirteenth month or an extended final close of the budget year is posted to the fiscal year that just closed. Only then can a determination be made whether the institution finished the fiscal year with a positive or negative budget balance. The effective budget manager knows and complies with these varied closing dates and understands the protocols of the institution regarding closing.

Analyzing the Results

When the budget cycle for the fiscal year is completed the results must be analyzed. Earlier in this chapter, it was noted that the first step in the budget cycle was to analyze past performance. Such analysis is also the last step in the budget cycle and is essential for success in budget management.

Unit budget managers should take the initiative to analyze the budget performance of their unit. This will allow the budget manager to answer questions about what happened during the last fiscal year and why it happened. If the budget plan failed to meet expectations or exceeded expectations, the reason(s) for the performance must be identified. The pattern could be repeated (either positively or negatively) if the causes are unknown. Questions should be asked regarding whether the performance was an anomaly or whether a trend in cost increases for certain line items can be identified and thus can be addressed in future budget requests. The answers to these and other questions will help the budget manager develop future budget requests and also answer any inquiries about future budget performance.

While unit budget managers are analyzing results and determining causation, an analysis is also going forward at the institutional level. Depending on the size and complexity of the institution such an analysis may be quite detailed and time consuming or it may be provided at a more gross level. In either case, the end result of the institutional budget analysis will initially result in two types of data: a report on the results of the year and an analysis of the variance in performance from the budget plan.

Reporting results is usually fairly straightforward and answers the question of how the institution or specific units performed during the last fiscal year. Did the institution deficit spend? Were all of the debt obligations met? What was the final outcome for the year and did it result in a positive or negative balance? Once the institution determines that the financial data are correct, a report is prepared by the institution and reviewed by external auditors. The governing board, the administration, government agencies, and other funding sources use the final audited report of performance to understand the financial status of the institution. The purpose of the external audit is not to analyze budget performance but to assure that the fiscal data are accurate and that the institution followed proper procedures and accounting standards over the last fiscal year. The audited financial report evaluates performance data from the prior fiscal year to the fiscal year under review for purposes of comparison, but an audited financial report does not provide the critical data needed for governance and administration of the institution.

In contrast, the internal institutional budget analysis, which focuses on the variance between the budget plan and what actually happened over the last fiscal year, helps place the budget performance for the recently ended fiscal year within the context of the performance of the prior year and the budget plan for the next fiscal year. Once variances in performance are identified, the analysis focuses on the causes of the variance. It is at this point that the individual unit analysis conducted by the unit budget manager is very valuable. Usually budget managers are the individuals in the organization who can explain why there was a difference between the planned budget and actual budget performance. Although some variances such as an unanticipated new contract for the steamfitters union can easily be explained at the institutional level, many require information from unit budget managers.

Once the institutional analysis is completed (including the explanation between performance and the planned budget), a report is prepared for the governing board, key administrators, and budget managers. This report will provide guidance in monitoring the budget in the new fiscal year and may identify areas where adjustments need to be made in the current budget in order to more closely reflect the reality of revenue and expenditures faced by the institution.

Conclusion

The budget cycle in any institution of higher education is complex and requires a great deal of attention to detail. Anyone with budget management responsibility for any unit within the institution must clearly understand the institutional budget cycle and parameters. Once that is clearly understood the unit budget manager can develop internal guidelines for budget development and a schedule that allows plenty of time to meet institutional deadlines. Usually if an administrator has budget responsibility he or she is managing not only the current budget but also closing out the previous fiscal year and planning for the next fiscal year.

References

Dickeson, R. C. *Prioritizing Academic Programs and Services: Reallocating Resources to Achieve Strategic Balance* (2nd ed.). San Francisco: Jossey-Bass, 2010.

Goldstein, R. C. *College and University Budgeting: An Introduction for Faculty and Academic Administration.* (3rd ed.). Washington, D.C.: National Association of College and University Business Officers, 2005.

Woodard, D. Jr., and Von Destinon, M. "Budgeting and Fiscal Management." In M. J. Barr, M. Desler, and Associates (eds.), *Handbook of Student Affairs Administration* (2nd ed.). San Francisco: Jossey-Bass, 2006.

Reflection Questions

The following questions may be helpful to consider as a budget cycle begins or ends.

1. Did the unit close the last fiscal year without problems? If there were problems what were they, and how can they be avoided in the future?

2. What are the reasons for any variance between the budget of the last fiscal year and the actual performance of the unit? Are those conditions likely to occur in the next fiscal year?

3. What is the most efficient way to provide constant monitoring of budget expenditures?

4. What options exist within the institution if you are faced with an unanticipated and unbudgeted major expense?

5. Were the forecasts for revenue in the unit budget accurate? How could that forecasting be improved?

6. Where are the consistent problems in the unit budget regarding overexpenditures and why do they occur?

5

Understanding Auxiliary and Capital Budgets

Chapter Three included an overview of various types of budgets. This chapter focuses on two of those budget types: auxiliary budgets and capital budgets. Both are special cases. The budget for an auxiliary unit reflects the expectation that the unit is self-sustaining. A capital budget reflects the project for which it is intended to serve. Auxiliary units may at times have capital projects under way for which a capital budget is in place.

Auxiliary Budgets

Auxiliary units are substantially, if not completely, self-supporting with regard to budget. This is not to say that auxiliary units are free to operate as they please. On the contrary, auxiliaries typically must abide by the same institutional guidelines as other units when it comes to budgetary practices and policies such as compensation, purchasing, and human resources. Further, auxiliaries may be expected to generate revenues in excess of their expenses and the surplus used to support the operations of other units. Common examples include surpluses from bookstore operations being used to support student life programs or student scholarships or surpluses from housing being used to support campus security.

Auxiliary units are often service units. Why is that the case? Although all activities of a college or university can (and arguably should) be constructed in ways that promote learning and development, many sources of public funds such as state legislatures tend to focus their support on functions directly tied to the academic mission of the institution.

Although perhaps most commonly associated with administrative units, the concept of auxiliary enterprise is by no means exclusive to such units. It is increasingly common for institutions to expect that academic institutes, centers, and similar enterprises be self-sufficient with regard to budget. There are also institutions at which continuing education or the summer session are operated as auxiliaries.

Why are some units at an institution considered auxiliaries while others are not? Auxiliary units typically provide service to a readily identifiable subgroup of the campus population, and the benefits from the provision of that service are substantially restricted to the user group. Examples include students who make use of campus recreation facilities or programs, residents in campus housing, or members of the campus community accessing health care through the campus clinic. Many institutions embrace the philosophy that those users ought to directly bear the cost of the services through fees charged to them, and it is practical to charge fees to the users given that they are a discrete group within the overall campus population.

The remainder of this section addresses several important planning issues for budget managers working with auxiliary budgets. These issues include forecasting revenues and expenses, paying for institutional services and overhead, planning for maintenance, and budgeting for reserves.

Forecasting Revenues and Expenses

Accurately forecasting revenue and expenses is critically important in the development of any budget but particularly for auxiliary units, given their unique financial standing. One helpful technique in the process of developing revenue and expense forecasts is to review past performance for a period of three to five years. The rolling average over that period can be a useful starting point for forecasting revenue or expenses in the coming year (see Table 5.1).

It is not sufficient, however, to simply use an approximation of the rolling average as the forecast for the coming budget year. The budget manager must also consider what changes might be taking place in the operational environment that could have an impact on revenue in the coming year. Suppose that a local, large manufacturing firm plans to end its support of a tuition reimbursement benefit for its employees who have, in the past, used that benefit to take courses at Alpha University under a Continuing Education program The dean plans to provide information about alternative strategies for funding college studies to those employees currently enrolled as students in an effort to help them complete their certificate and degree plans, but it appears likely that enrollments from the manufacturing company's employees will decline. The revenue forecast for the coming year must reflect that likelihood (see Table 5.2).

Table 5.1.   Alpha University Continuing Education Revenue from Tuition and Fees

Actual Close Year 1	Actual Close Year 2	Actual Close Year 3	Actual Close Year 4	Projected Close Year 5	Forecasted Year 6
723,450	729,600	728,700	730,845	729,975	729,000

Table 5.2.   Alpha University Continuing Education Revenue from Tuition and Fees Accounting for Response to Local Manufacturer's Decision

Actual Close Year 1	Actual Close Year 2	Actual Close Year 3	Actual Close Year 4	Projected Close Year 5	Forecasted Year 6
723,450	729,600	728,700	730,845	729,975	644,000

Similarly, a budget manager must look beyond the simple rolling average and consider whether or not there are meaningful trends in the data that may inform the revenue forecast for the year ahead. Three years ago a for-profit business college opened near Alpha University, and last year the local community college began aggressively marketing its associate programs in office management and other business-related areas. Table 5.3 reflects the reality of the impact of these developments with no changes to Alpha's current fees or programs.

The leadership team of Alpha University's School of Continuing Education and appropriate members of the institution's leadership might decide to launch a new alumni college program designed to increase alumni enrollment in its pay-for-service mini-courses as a means to help offset enrollment losses to the for-profit institution and community college. Another idea being considered is to develop and market language education programs in languages such as Chinese and Korean, which are not taught in local high schools or at other smaller institutions in the area. It would be unwise to make unrealistic assumptions about the impact of these two new efforts in the first year of their implementation, but the budget manager believes that at a minimum the initiatives will stabilize the situation. The revenue for the coming year is forecast accordingly (see Table 5.4).

Although we have chosen in this section to use examples related to forecasting revenue, the same technique and caveats can be applied to forecasting expenses.

Table 5.3.   Alpha University Continuing Education Revenue from Tuition and Fees Accounting for Increased Local Competition

Actual Close Year 1	Actual Close Year 2	Actual Close Year 3	Actual Close Year 4	Projected Close Year 5	Forecasted Year 6
723,450	720,200	720,700	698,845	683,975	678,500

Table 5.4.   Alpha University Continuing Education Revenue from Tuition and Fees Reflecting Two New Initiatives

Actual Close Year 1	Actual Close Year 2	Actual Close Year 3	Actual Close Year 4	Projected Close Year 5	Forecasted Year 6
723,450	720,200	720,700	698,845	683,975	685,500

Paying for Institutional Services and Overhead

Auxiliary units are required to pay for the services they receive from the institution. Charges for such services typically take one of two forms: direct or fee-for-service charges and general charge back.

The direct or fee-for service model is used when it is practical to determine specific charges for the service rendered. A common example of this model is physical plant services. The auxiliary unit is charged for the actual services rendered by tradesmen such as carpenters, electricians, or plumbers by using a ticketing system that shows the time and materials used for a specific job. Some units may be large enough that tradesmen are assigned by the institution exclusively to the unit, but the unit is charged for the work they actually do based on a ticketing system.

A general charge model is appropriate when it would be difficult to discern a discrete service act upon which to base billing to the auxiliary. Take for example the case of police services. There is little doubt that campus housing draws considerably on the services of campus police, but it would be challenging if not impossible to develop a fee-for-service billing for that relationship. Instead an institution will assess a general charge to housing for its use of police services. That charge is calculated as a percentage of the unit's expenses based on an established formula.

Whether employing fee-for-service or general charge back, wise budget managers will be as careful in reviewing internal charges for service as they are in monitoring charges from external vendors. Such reviews assure the accuracy of billing to the unit and can provide helpful insights into operational performance that can lead to future savings. For example, the budget manager for Alpha University's residence halls notices that there are charges every year from Printing Services for the production of banners for recurring events such as move-in weekend. The budget manager follows up with a member of the professional staff in residence life, and together they determine that the banners could be reused if references to the year were to be removed. That decision results in a savings of several hundred dollars a year to the residence life budget.

In addition to charges for services directly received by the unit, it is common practice for auxiliaries to be charged an overhead fee to support the general operation of the institution. Revenue from these fees fund units such as accounting, bursar, and purchasing. Like the general charge for direct services, the overhead fee is usually the function of a formula established by the institution that reflects a percentage of the auxiliary unit's expenses. The budget manager for an auxiliary should be familiar with the way in which the overhead fee is determined.

Planning for Maintenance

It is very important that auxiliary units have plans in place to address their ongoing maintenance needs given that the cost of that maintenance is borne by the unit as opposed to being spread across the institution, as is the case for units supported through the appropriated operating budget of the institution. Carpets, painting, furniture, computers, and software are just a few examples of the assets of a unit that must be regularly replaced or updated.

Auxiliary units should develop a maintenance cycle by "establishing a list of items to be repaired or refurbished and then establishing a life cycle for each item" (McClellan and Barr, 2000, p. 203). The carpet in a four-story student union may need to be replaced every four years, and the budget may reflect the intention to replace carpeting on one floor each year. Public printers in the residence halls commons may need to be replaced every other year, translating to a budget that allows for replacement of half of the printers annually.

In addition to developing a maintenance cycle for routine ongoing maintenance and budgeting accordingly, auxiliary units with facilities must also plan for the replacement of major building infrastructure such as roofs, plumbing, or electrical systems. These items do not need to be replaced with the same frequency as items such as carpets or departmental vehicles, but they do have a life expectancy that can be used to estimate the period of time over which funds for replacement can be accumulated. An auxiliary then includes in its budget an annualized expense for deferred maintenance, and those funds are typically transferred to reserve accounts to accumulate until they are needed.

It can be tempting, and indeed at times even necessary, to forgo funding routine maintenance or deferred maintenance. However, doing so is simply "kicking the can down the road" and will lead to more critical budgeting problems for the unit in the future.

Budgeting for Reserves

As noted above, auxiliary units typically include an expense for deferred maintenance in their annual budgets. Those funds are typically transferred annually to a dedicated reserve account as part of the process budget cycle, with the transfers being either mandatory or discretionary in accordance with institutional policies. The funds accumulated over the years in that reserve account are then available for use for major deferred maintenance projects.

Accumulating funds for deferred maintenance is not the only reason to develop reserves. Auxiliary units may also access reserve funds to address unanticipated challenges or opportunities. The university's basketball team may qualify for the national tournament, and athletics may wish to offer transportation to take cheerleaders and the pep band with the team. A grease fire in the kitchen of one of the food service units on campus may necessitate cleanup, repainting, equipment replacement, and the recharging of the fire alarm system. Whereas those expenses will eventually be reimbursed through the institution's insurance, the food service is expected to pay the expenses up front. Having a modest reserve on hand can be a source of great comfort, and the prudent budget manager for an auxiliary unit will work to assure that transfers to reserves cover the annualized cost for deferred maintenance, as well as some additional portion for the unanticipated but seemingly inevitable events that occur.

Capital Budgets

Price (2009) observes that "Along with personnel and financial resources, facilities are one of the main tools we have as professionals to achieve our programmatic goals" (p. 565). The argument can certainly be extended to include all of higher education. It is not surprising then that expenditures for the construction or renovation of facilities in higher education are substantial. One survey of 470 institutions found that as a group they spent 14.5 billion dollars in 2005 on such projects (Akel, 2006).

"Construction of new facilities and renovation of existing facilities present some of the most complicated fiscal problems in higher education" (Barr, 1988, p. 28). Capital budgets are created for the purpose of supporting such construction or renovation. Capital budgets typically include expenses for design, including architectural services and engineering services. Usually there are costs associated with studying the site to assure its suitability as a location for the building being considered. The budget will also include charges for the various trades, as well as liability insurance associated with the project. It may also include site preparation and landscaping expenses. The capital budget is likely to include expenses related to materials for carpeting, finishes, fixtures, and painting, but it may or may not include funds for furnishings, depending on the institutional practice associated with assigning those costs to either the capital or operating budget. Table 5.5 offers an example of a capital budget for a construction project.

Table 5.5. Capital Budget for Alpha University Project

Expense	Original Budget	Changes	Revised Budget	Commitment	Expenditures	Available
Office	3,066	0	3,066	0	2,107	959
Printing/ duplicating	1,000	0	1,000	0	459	541
General contract	506,700	18,370	525,070	322,710	202,360	0
Architectural/ engineering fees	34,500	0	34,500	9,500	25,000	0
Supervision	21,940	0	21,940	10,265	11,675	0
Landscaping	25,000	1,250	26,250	26,250	0	0
Insurance	410	0	410	0	410	0
Project management	37,614	0	37,614	19,790	17,824	0
Contingency	40,536	0	40,536	19,620	0	20,916
Total	670,766	19,620	690,386	408,135	259,835	22,416

This section discusses issues associated with capital budgets. The issues include the relationship between planning and capital budgets, funding capital projects, the impact of social issues on capital budgets, and the need to watch out in the budgeting process for the possibility of hidden costs. The chapter concludes with questions for reflection.

Planning and Capital Budgets

Like all budget forms, capital budgets should "flow naturally from good planning—good planning does not emanate from adequate budgets" (Boyle, 1995, p. 52). Planning for a capital project should be an inclusive process and include advisory board members, representatives from user groups (including students), staff members from units that are housed in or make substantial use of the facility, and management team members (McClellan and Barr, 2000). In some cases, it may also be advisable to include members of the broader community.

A critical step in the planning of a capital project is the development of a program statement. A program statement describes what will go on in the new facility, how the parts of the new facility need to relate to one another, the number and types of people it will serve, and what units will be occupants. The work of McClellan and Barr (2000) and Price (2003, 2009) may be helpful to readers interested in learning more about program statements for capital projects.

Just as participation in the planning process should be inclusive, so too should the considerations for the impact of the project on the budgets of units housed in the facility or making substantial use of the facility, units in areas of campus near the project, and on the overall budget of the institution. How will the new project affect usage of programs and services, and what are the implications for staffing? Will the new facility change traffic patterns on campus in ways that necessitate changes in security patrols or safety resources such as emergency phones or lighting? What impact will the inclusion of a coffee shop have on the vending proceeds in other buildings?

Groups involved in the planning of a capital project often find themselves in a "chicken-and-egg scenario" (Price, 2009, p. 569). Should they plan for what they can fund, or should they seek to fund what they plan? The former may limit the possibilities of the project; the latter may lead to delays in initiating the project pending the securing of funds or to complications late in the project when cuts in the plan have to be made quickly because the necessary funding fails to materialize.

One strategy for addressing the dilemma identified by Price is to begin by pursuing a process of what the Walt Disney Company refers to as "Imagineering" ("Walt Disney Imagineering," Wikipedia). In considering new projects, the Disney team begins project development by imagining what they would like the project to be and then considering how that imaginative vision might be engineered. Mills' (2003) construct of value engineering is a helpful model in higher education. Value engineering is a collaborative effort of representatives from the institution as well as firms involved in the design, development, and construction of the project with the goal of that effort being to make informed decisions regarding features of the project that will allow the greatest realization of the imagined possibility while adhering to the practical reality of the budget available.

Funding Capital Budgets

The practical reality of a capital budget is defined by the funding available to support it. McClellan and Barr (2000) identify several strategies for financing new construction.

Self-Financing

It is common practice for institutions to include in operating budgets a sum to be transferred to capital reserves to fund ongoing and deferred maintenance. Institutions may also elect to self-finance capital projects by lending funding to the project from an institutional source, often the institution's endowment. That loan must be repaid with interest, and the budget for the operation of the facility must include the cost of servicing that debt.

One might wonder why the institution would elect to charge itself interest, but to do otherwise would be a failure of fiduciary responsibility. Were the institution not to use the funds for the project, it would be in a position to benefit from the investment of those funds.

Another self-funding strategy for building capital reserves is earmarking some portion of revenue from endowments for the purposes of a capital project. However, fluctuations in the investment market can present challenges to institutions that rely heavily on such income to fund the costs of the inexorable depreciation of significant capital assets.

The advantages to an institution of self-financing a capital project include the freedom to move forward with the project and advantageous financing when compared to financing available from other sources. Of course, an institution must first have available funds sufficient to support the project and sufficient additional funds to assure continuity of operation once the project funds are committed.

Gift Support

Institutions may also seek support for capital projects from donors. Donors may be individuals or philanthropic organizations, and few projects are fully funded by a single donor. Typically a project will have a major gift that anchors the funding, and the facility is often named in honor of the donor providing that major gift. Additional naming opportunities can be available for rooms or other features throughout a facility.

It is not uncommon for large donations to be paid to the institution over a period of time. The budget for a capital project will need to account for the schedule of donor pledge payments.

Bonds

Institutions sometimes have unmet need for resources for a capital project. One option for addressing that need is through the issuance of bonds subject to the institution's legal authority to do so.

Bonds are a form of debt. The institution receives funds up front from the sale of the bonds and promises to make repayment with interest at some defined point in the future. The repayment is funded through future revenues. In the case of auxiliaries those revenues may include the assessment of user fees, including mandatory or optional fees for students (see Chapter Two for discussion of such fees). The repayment cost of a bond issuance is the face value of the bonds, the interest paid on them, and the cost of issuing them.

The authority to issue bonds for sale typically rests with the governing board of the institution, and public institutions or systems are sometimes restricted by law to a maximum ceiling for total bond indebtedness. Private institutions may have policies with similar effect.

Why would such limits be placed on institutions of higher education, which, as a group, are incredibly stable economic enterprises and seen as relatively safe investments? Like any individual or institution the more debt one carries in relation to income the lower the credit rating for that individual or institution. The financial health of an institution affects its bond rating, which in turn affects the costs of attracting investors in future bond issuances. It may also have an impact on other financial considerations, such as short-term loans to meet operating expenses while waiting for tuition revenue to arrive or the faith that a potential donor has in an institution's management of its resources.

The attractiveness of an institution's bonds in the marketplace is largely a function of the institution's credit worthiness as reflected in the rating it has from major commercial credit rating agencies such as Moody's or Standard and Poor's (S&P). Table 5.6 describes the rating structures for these two agencies.

Table 5.6. Moody's and S&P Ratings

Moody's		S&P	
Aaa	Highest quality; minimal risk	AAA	Highest rating; extremely strong capacity to meet financial commitments
Aa	High quality; very low risk	AA	Only slightly below AAA
A	Upper-medium grade; low risk	A	Strong capacity to meet financial commitments but somewhat vulnerable to adverse circumstance or changing conditions
Baa	Medium grade; moderate risk	BBB	Adequate capacity to meet financial commitments; adverse circumstances or changing conditions more likely to lead to weakened capacity
Ba	Speculative; substantial risk	BB	Less vulnerable than others rated lower but facing major uncertainties; adverse circumstances or conditions could lead to inability or unwillingness to meet commitments
B	Speculative; substantial risk	B	More vulnerable than BB; currently can meet commitments but conditions or changes are likely to impair ability or willingness to meet obligations
Caa	Poor; high risk	CCC	Vulnerable; reliant on favorable conditions to meet commitments
Ca	Highly speculative, likely to be in or near default	CC	Highly vulnerable to not meet commitments
C	Lowest rating; typically in default	C	Highly vulnerable and perhaps headed to bankruptcy
		D	In default

Adapted from Stripling (2009).

External agencies from time to time make a review visit to an institution as part of developing their credit rating for that institution. Such reviews, like external reviews from accrediting bodies, require extensive and careful preparation and the efforts of numerous individuals and offices. Coordination of the preparation process should occur through one central authority for the institution. Usually a unit budget manager will only be peripherally involved in such reviews but may be asked to provide information or prepare reports used for the review.

Appropriations

Institutions may also be able to fund capital projects through appropriations from either state or federal sources. Price (2009) notes that such appropriations are often for academic buildings rather than other types.

Joint Ventures

An increasingly common strategy for institutions to fund capital projects is to enter into joint ventures. These ventures often support capital projects related to auxiliary activities. The institution typically makes available the land and commits to the operation as an institutional activity; the private partner provides funding for construction (and sometimes start-up operations) and may be contracted to provide management services for the operation once the facility is open. One model for structuring these joint ventures is for a separate 501(c)(3) corporation to be established for the purposes of constructing and operating the facility. This arrangement is particularly advantageous for public institutions in that it allows the project to sidestep myriad regulations related to the development and construction of public projects and thereby help expedite the project and lower costs.

It is important to note that any consideration of seeking external funding for capital projects, like seeking external funding for other institutional purposes, should be coordinated with

the appropriate institutional offices such as development and officers such as the chief executive. Such coordination helps assure
that the institution presents itself in a consistent fashion to outside funding sources and that the best request is made to them by
the institution.

Social Changes and Capital Budgets

The design of capital projects is influenced by campus environments, which are in turn influenced by the broader society
(McClellan and Barr, 2000). Projects being considered for campuses must take into account issues of diversity, high expectations,
integration of technology, and community. Institutions are unlikely
to design and build traditional residence halls with double-loaded
linear corridors and community baths in an era when students have
increasing expectations with regard to privacy and room features.
The new technological standard for academic buildings includes
smart classrooms with wireless access. Campuses are focused on
creating a sense of community, and one way they pursue that focus
is through inclusion of welcoming community-gathering spaces in
buildings across campus.

Legal requirements for accessible facilities, services, and programs are an example of a social concern that can have profound
implications on the budget for a capital budget. In addition, institutional aspirations to exceed legal requirements for accessibility
may add to construction costs for all types of campus buildings.

The "green" movement is another social change that is commonly reflected in construction and renovation projects on college campuses (Akel, 2006), but the increased costs in the capital
budgets of such projects may be offset by reductions in ongoing
costs through savings in expenses for utilities (Martin and Samels,
2006; Price, 2009). Environmentally responsive and sustainable
capital projects may also be able to attract funding through grants
dedicated to supporting such development or through gifts from
donors interested in "green" issues.

Note that responding to social issues might have an impact on more than just the capital budget for the construction or renovation project. It may also have implications for the ongoing operational or auxiliary budget of the units in the facility, as there may be ongoing additional staffing needs or increased maintenance costs.

Watch Out for Hidden Costs

Be it for construction or renovation, it is important that the capital budget be able to absorb the unforeseen or hidden costs that emerge in the course of the project. Costs in construction can be negatively affected by zoning disputes, labor actions, or unanticipated environmental issues in site preparation.

Costs can also be negatively affected by change orders—changes in design specifications made once the project is under way. Change orders typically result in additional charges to the project. Although the expense of a few change orders is typically assumed for any project and built into the contingency line of the budget, the costs of numerous change orders are not. One of the surest strategies for minimizing change orders on a project is the thoughtful and thorough development of a program statement.

Just as inadequate planning can lead to increased costs, capital budgets for major renovations can also suffer as a result of a lack of accurate information regarding the condition of building infrastructure hidden behind walls, unanticipated asbestos abatement, or belated notification that the project will trigger the necessity to upgrade building features to bring them into code compliance. The older the building the more prone the project is to such problems. The importance of accurate architectural plans for the building being renovated cannot be overstated, and it may be a worthwhile investment to spend money in having such plans verified and updated prior to the project rather than responding to problems resulting from their inaccuracies or inadequacies during the project.

As noted earlier, the budget manager must assure the capital budget includes sufficient funds to address such contingencies. However, this must be balanced with the need not to be so conservative regarding contingency budgeting that approval for the project is jeopardized or money is wasted through borrowing more for the project than is required. Once the project is approved and under way, the budget manager and others involved in managing the project must stay in close communication in order to assure that the project stays on budget and to respond to problems or opportunities as they appear (Price, 2003).

Conclusion

The role of the budget manager is critically important to the success of his or her unit and institution. This chapter presented information on some of the unique considerations for the budget manager working with auxiliary units or capital projects. Though both are special cases in higher education budgeting, a common theme for both is the importance of careful planning and proactive management.

References

Akel, M. "A Greener Attitude." University Business, September 2006. [http://www.universitybusiness.com/viewarticle.aspx?articleid=549]. Accessed on December 10, 2009.

Barr, M. J. "Managing the Enterprise." In M. L. Upcraft and M. J. Barr (Eds.), Managing Student Affairs Effectively. San Francisco: Jossey-Bass, 1988.

Boyle, T. P. "Good Questions for Sound Decision Making." In D. W. Woodard (Ed.), Budgeting as a Tool for Policy in Student Affairs. San Francisco: Jossey-Bass, 1995.

Martin, J., and Samels, J. E. "A New Breed of American Energy Colleges and Universities." University Business, September 2006. [http://www.universitybusiness.com/viewarticle.aspx?articleid=630]. Accessed on December 10, 2009.

McClellan, G. S., and Barr, M. J. "Planning, Managing, and Financing Facilities and Services." In M. J. Barr and M. K. Desler (Eds.), *The Handbook of Student Affairs Administration* (2nd ed.). San Francisco: Jossey-Bass, 2000.

Mills, D. B. "Assembling the Project Team." In. J. M. Price (Ed.), *Planning and Achieving Successful Student Affairs Facilities Projects*. New Directions for Student Services, no. 101. San Francisco: Jossey-Bass, 2003.

Price, J. M. "From First Design Brainstorm in Session to Final Coat of Paint: Communication, an Essential Constant." In. J. M. Price (Ed.), *Planning and Achieving Successful Student Affairs Facilities Projects*. New Directions for Student Services, no. 101. San Francisco: Jossey-Bass, 2003.

Price, J. M. "Planning and Development." In G. S. McClellan and J. Stringer (Eds.), *The Handbook of Students Affairs Administration* (3rd ed.). San Francisco: Jossey-Bass, 2009.

"Walt Disney Imagineering." Wikipedia [http://en.wikipedia.org/wiki/Walt_Disney_Imagineering]

Reflection Questions

1. What are the auxiliary units on your campus? Are they expected to be fully self-supporting, or do they receive some funding from other sources?

2. What would a good schedule for regular maintenance for facilities under your supervision look like?

3. What is your institution's credit rating? Has the rating changed in the past several years? If so, what factors may have led to an increase or decrease in your institution's credit rating? Why is the change important?

4. What legal mandates have influenced the construction of new facilities on your campus in recent years?

5. How have the campus environment and social changes shaped recent construction or renovation projects on your campus? What impact do you imagine that to have had on the capital budgets associated with those projects?

6

Problems and Pitfalls in Budget
Management

Although Chapter Four, on the budget cycle(s), approaches the issues of budget management as a rational process with steps that everyone follows and guidelines that everyone adheres to, it is usually a much more complex than that and can be much more confusing. Politics, people, publicity, and problem areas can all influence the development of an institutional budget. For example, if there has been a series of incidents on the campus regarding safety of students that has received a great deal of publicity, then new support for campus safety may become part of the budget of the institution. Or if an elected representative (at either the state or federal level) has an interest in public transportation, then an appropriation might come to a state institution for expansion of the Traffic Management Institute that provides training to local and state law enforcements officers. These things can happen even if the campus public safety budget is already robust and the institution is not interested in expanding the range and scope of the Traffic Management Institute. In addition, if a flood occurs in the basement of the library and results in major expenses to restore part of the library collection, there will certainly be an unexpected addition to the budget. If a budget manager-administrator is able to anticipate most problems and develop solutions, then the unusual or the unexpected will be much easier to handle. This chapter is designed to help budget managers avoid common pitfalls in budget management. The advice in this chapter is drawn from the combined wisdom of fiscal managers, fiscal staff, and executive staff members at both public and private institutions. We hope that their collective wisdom will aid unit budget managers at all levels in the institution in becoming more effective in their role.

The chapter first describes the common issues faced by budget managers. Second, it addresses the common pitfalls in budget and fiscal management. Third, it provides collective advice to new or less experienced budget managers. Finally, the chapter focuses on the attitude of the budget manager-administrator and the differ-ence attitude can make for success in that role.

Common Issues

There are a number of common issues facing budget managers, particularly managers who are relatively new to those responsibili-ties. Among them are

- Understanding the unit organization and the decision-making processes that effect the unit
- Understanding the history of decision making in the unit
- Assessing the capabilities of colleagues within the unit
- Identifying chronic and one-time problems within the unit that need to be solved
- The political and personal issues involved in managing change within the unit

All can be frustrating, but all must be addressed.

Understanding the Organization

In order to function effectively budget administrators (whether faculty or staff) need to understand the unit for which they are responsible and the larger institution, and how they interact. Such understanding does not come easily and requires initiative and investment of time on the part of the budget manager. Most academic, business, and student affairs administrators understand that learning about their unit is extremely important. Understanding internal procedures, decision-making structures, and the way business has been done in the past within the unit is a first step toward success. However, paying attention only to the unit can become a trap. Often budget managers focus so much on learning about their own unit that important connections are not made to potential partners in and the issues of the larger institution.

Successful budget managers need to extend their understanding of the formal organizational chart and be able "to identify the individuals, communication links, and alliances that never appear on paper. This extended organizational structure is usually identified through careful observation, informal conversations and tracking how decisions are made" (Barr, 1985, p. 71). By taking the time to understand the larger organization, budget managers can identify a number of people within the institution who can help them be successful in their budget management role. Each department or division is different, but key contacts in accounting, budgeting, purchasing, information technology, and physical plant are usually essential for any budgetary unit in a college or university. Becoming more than a voice on the phone is invaluable if there is a problem to be solved or information that is needed.

In addition to getting answers to specific questions, these contacts provide valuable "soft data" that can assist the budget manager. Asking questions of those who work directly with the budget manager's department and finding out what kinds of requests or actions from members of your unit frustrated those working in other parts of the institution is valuable information that can assist in avoiding problems and issues.

Finally, a network of colleagues across the institution helps budget managers set reasonable expectations for their colleagues within the unit and across the institution. For example, knowing how long it really takes to get a purchase order processed or a budget transfer made can help everyone plan their own work more effectively. Finding out who should be called if there has been an accounting mistake or a purchase order delay can help any budget manager be more efficient and effective.

Understanding the Budget History of the Unit

Each budget manager approaches that task in a unique way and develops internal processes and structures that are consistent with his or her management style and approach to problem solving. For success as a new budget manager it is essential to understand the mores regarding the budget and financial management that were the former standards within the unit. Some units have a history of very tight control in which all expenditures are approved by the unit budget manager. Others have a system whereby expenditures can be made up to a certain dollar amount without the approval of the budget manager. Such practices have become part of the organizational culture, and if budget managers do not understand those practices, there is great potential for miscommunication and confusion.

To illustrate, a new vice president had a meeting with her unit heads and distributed the budget guidelines from the institution and the internal budget guidelines for the division. The packets for each unit head also included budget forms and other back-up materials. After distribution she looked around the table and saw consternation on the faces of the unit heads. As she questioned the reaction, slowly but surely she began to understand that the unit heads had never before been asked to participate in building the budget request from the division—it had all been done by the vice president. A great deal of additional assistance was needed during that first year to help the department heads feel comfortable as they prepared budget documents. Even after the budget was submitted additional time was invested with some unit managers to increase their confidence as direct budget managers. If the new vice president had understood the history of the division, preparation could have occurred earlier in the year with training implemented to help department heads deal with their new budget management responsibilities.

Any budget manager must also gain a full understanding of all accounts and revenue sources that are part of the financial plan for the unit. Assumptions should not be made about the validity of the current budget or the uses made for reserve funds (if applicable). Rather, budget managers should examine the financial records for the program or department and ask questions so that problems can be identified before they become major concerns.

For example, a review of the unit budget performance in the prior fiscal year (see Chapter Four) revealed that there was substantial variance between the budgeted line item for computer supplies and the actual expenditures in the line. Finding out why that occurred is important. If the response from those involved is "We have always done it that way and just transfer funds from another line to cover it" then there is a budget problem that needs to be solved.

Understanding the budget history of the unit also means that the budget manager will be able to create a list of issues that must be addressed and problems that must be solved. Priorities for addressing the issues involved can be established. All issues cannot be addressed in one fiscal year but progress can be made. In addition, process and procedures that work can be identified and continued. Spending time to understand what was inherited is essential preparation for becoming much more effective in the budget manager role.

Assessing Capabilities

A budget manager must also be able to effectively assess the financial capabilities of colleagues within the unit. The budget is straightforward and easy to manage for some units, and support needs for the budget manager within the unit are minimal. In other units, managing the budget involves multiple accounts and sources of revenue, as well as reserve funds and capital projects. If the budget in the department or program is complex, one of the first steps to take is to assess the capabilities of department or unit members in handling financial matters. Are there individuals in the unit who handle purchasing and routine financial matters very well? Are there individuals who cannot seem to focus on matters financial? Each colleague within the budget unit will have strengths and weaknesses, and an assessment of their financial skills and capabilities must be made prior to granting them authority in matters financial. Identify who within the department or program expresses interest in finance and budgeting. Who among the faculty and staff in the department is open to new ideas and change? A bright and competent person can be trained in fiscal matters and become an asset to the entire organization.

In addition, self-assessment is needed. Examining your own capabilities and identifying your strengths and opportunities for improving your performance are very important. Even if there are not formal staff development programs at the institution on matters of budget and finance, wise managers identify what they need to know and seek help from others within the institution to acquire the needed skills, information, and competencies.

Identifying Problems and Developing Solutions

As mentioned earlier, the greatest skill that a financial manager can have is the ability to anticipate genuine problems before they become crises. Regular and routine budget reviews are invaluable to the process of problem identification. In addition, a retrospective review of past budgets and unit performance can help pinpoint chronic issues that must be addressed in the unit. It is important to differentiate between chronic budget problems (which require long-term solutions) and minor issues that can be addressed by immediate changes in policies and procedures.

Chronic budget and financial problems usually are not easily solved. For example, in some situations, one program within the department consistently goes into debt because the original budget to support the effort was not realistic. Other programs and general line items within the department have been used to cover the program deficit. As costs for supplies and services rise, using these resources as a strategy becomes less and less viable. Further, the chronic deficit has reduced the amount of money available to be transferred to equipment reserves for use by the entire department. This situation is illustrative of a chronic problem. The pattern of overspending has been firmly established, and staff members in the program in question have begun to expect other programs within the department to cover the deficit. There are both negative attitudes and fiscal realities to confront. In this case, the unit budget manager must develop both a short-term and long-term approach to solving the problem. The short-term solution might be to discuss the overspending issue with the director of the program that is chronically in deficit and jointly establish a reduced target spending goal for the program. The long-term solution might be to submit a special budget request for additional support outlining the original cause of the problem and evaluation data that supports the program effectiveness. Another solution might be to assess all program offerings of the unit to determine whether any can be dropped, modified, or consolidated. A third solution might be to ask the specific program staff to generate ideas to assure that budget performance within their area improves. A fourth solution might be to develop a new revenue source for the program. Each of these strategies should be tested within the unit and cannot be unilaterally adopted. Consultation must also be held with appropriate colleagues in the institution regarding the intended and unintended consequences of the chosen strategy.

If the problem is a chronic one, then the unit budget manager will also need to seek assistance from the institutional central budget office or officer. Lay out the problem and alternative solutions explored within the department and ask them for their advice and input with regard to the best solution for the specific issue. The broad-based expertise of the central budget office often will be enormously helpful in solving the problems faced in the unit. The best approach is to be forthright about the problem and not to ignore it. If the budget manager is clear and direct in communications with staff in the central budget office, credibility will be established with that office that will be useful in the future.

When problems do arise (and they will), the relationships the wise budget manager has developed are great resources to help solve the problem. Others who have faced similar issues can share possible solutions and expertise, and those perspectives are very useful in choosing a strategy to solve the problem. In the future, the budget manager who sought help can help others address the issues they face. One of the key requisites for management success is to discover what other people did under similar circumstances and what the patterns of response in the institution were to those decisions.

Managing Change

One of the most difficult issues that a manager faces is the management of change. Whether the proposed change is large or small, it is guaranteed to create resistance and concern within the budget unit. Barr and Golseth (1990) developed three guiding principles for managing change that are particularly useful for the financial manager: determining issues of agreement and commonality, demonstrating integrity, and demonstrating utility (pp. 209–210).

The principle of establishing commonality is particularly important in managing fiscal change. Try to identify answers to the following questions:

- What are the issues that frustrate people within the budget unit?

- What is working well?
- What needs to be modified?

Broad and open discussions within the budget unit will reveal common questions of concern and also identify those processes and procedures that do *not* need to be fixed. Such dialogue should be ongoing within a budget unit, for consistent attention to problem solving will stop small problems from becoming a crisis. Finally, if members of the unit become invested in the process of developing solutions to problems and their input is valued, they are much more likely to support change.

Integrity is essential to a positive change strategy within a budget unit. Demonstrating integrity is a simple but powerful practice that guides the ethical dimension of budget management. "Integrity involves principles that are assumed rather than affirmed. Integrity means demonstrating consistency between beliefs and actions" (Barr and Golseth, 1990, p. 210). For the budget manager, integrity in managing change is essential. Complete agreement on the changes needed is not always necessary, but everyone involved in the process of change must be treated with respect and honesty. The principle of integrity means that the budget manager must demonstrate consistency and fairness in all matters related to fiscal management, including the process of change.

The last principle in managing change is that of utility. Is the change worth doing? What is gained if the change is made? What is lost? Who benefits? Is it worth time and energy to make the change or is it making a "mountain out of a molehill?" Utility is an important principle in managing fiscal change. Often elaborate solutions to a problem are developed when it is just an anomaly that occurred one time and will never be repeated, or money-saving ideas are introduced that actually cost money because of the need for very specialized record keeping. When managing change one of the first questions to ask is whether the change is really needed and whether it is worth the time and energy involved in the process. A rule to remember is that everything seems to work better when it is simple and easy to understand. As one financial manager indicates, the wise budget manager "works with the hand that is dealt to them and phases in change" (E. Wachtel, personal communication, July 2001).

Many organizational theorists have studied the process of change, but space limitations do not allow full coverage of the topic here. Readers interested in more on this topic should see the work of Argyris and Schön (1978), Baldridge (1971), Bolman and Deal (2003), and Schneider (1990).

Common Pitfalls

There are a number of pitfalls that cause problems for budget managers. These pitfalls can be avoided with foresight and perspective. In this section nine pitfalls in budget management are identified and discussed.

Reliance on Handshake Deals

Lots of important work at a college or university is done informally without long memorandums of understanding and commitment. These informal agreements, sometimes called "handshake deals," are part of the fabric of decision making in most colleges and universities, and many positive outcomes can result from informal arrangements. Agreements regarding financial matters, however, should always be followed up with an e-mail, a memo, or some other written communication that clearly stipulates the financial agreement that has been made. Failure to document informal agreements does three things:

1. It allows misperceptions about the agreement to continue. Hence, subsequent decisions may be made on faulty assumptions.

2. It relies on individuals' memory instead of a firm agreement of mutual financial obligations.

3. The original handshake agreement can be forgotten as leadership changes within the institution or the budget unit.

So do not rely on handshake agreements—back them up with specific written descriptions of the agreement.

Overestimating Revenue

The most common mistake is to overestimate revenue for the unit. Revenue estimates should always be conservative and clearly articulate the assumptions for the stated revenue goal. Sometimes revenue is overestimated because the budget manager and the program staff are enthusiastic and optimistic about participation and response to a new idea for a program. That enthusiasm clouds the hard fiscal judgments that must be made. In addition, one-time revenue from a lecture or conference can be mistakenly projected as an ongoing source of funds for the next fiscal year. Finally, revenue calculations can be inflated because of simple arithmetic errors or faulty assumptions about the future of the program or the amount of support that will continue from the institution. Whatever the reason, failure to accurately estimate revenue will cause problems down the road. Remember that conservative revenue estimates are the foundation of sound budgeting.

Postponing a Problem

Sometimes it feels like the easiest course of action is to do nothing. The problem has been present in the unit for some time and everyone has learned to work around it. Why rock the boat? There are situations when avoidance is a reasonable strategy, including when there are other more pressing issues that must be resolved, but often avoidance only causes the problem to grow. If there is great variance between expected budget performance for the unit and what is actually happening, then there is a problem that must be addressed. Deficits do not vanish, and overexpenditures do not melt away. For illustration, some time ago someone, somewhere in the institution agreed that the Political Science Department could run a modest deficit (not defined) in the line supporting the annual Midwest Graduate Student Symposium on Contemporary Issues in Political Science. The conference has been held every year for the past ten years, and the deficit from the symposium has been absorbed each year by the Political Science Department. During this last year the deficit related to the conference grew to a substantial amount that could not be absorbed by the department. The budget manager was faced with a problem that had to be solved, and ignoring the problem for so many years had allowed it to grow into a larger issue.

Sometimes the solution can be found within the unit. Sometimes help is needed from elsewhere in the institution. That was the case for the Political Science Department. The Arts and Sciences dean eventually covered the deficit but not without an admonition that the symposium could not run a deficit in the future. The budget manager for political science worked with the faculty involved to find other support for the symposium, including a grant from a foundation, and the event was moved to a biannual gathering rather than an annual one. Whatever was needed, the financial manager for the unit had to find a solution.

Failing to Ask for Help

Fear of looking foolish is no excuse for not asking for help when it is needed. The greatest skill that administrators with financial responsibilities can have is recognizing an issue before it becomes a larger problem. The second greatest skill is asking for help to solve the problem. Help is available from all sorts of sources within the institution, including fellow budget managers and members of the central financial staff. Wasting time and energy in trying to solve the problem without seeking expert help from others is foolish, and the solution that is developed may not be optimal. Asking for help is simply a strong management strategy.

Failing to Identify Hidden Costs

All programs have hidden as well as visible costs. Hidden costs may involve the expense of renting space, utility charges for new program spaces, or furniture and equipment provided for all program spaces, and sometimes such costs are not addressed when budget proposals to support new programs are presented. Any hidden costs must be identified and accounted for in a program financial plan. It is only when all such costs are known that a rational decision can be made about investing in the new program. Capital budgeting requires that operational costs for new facilities be identified and accounted for in the financial plan (see Chapter Five for further information), but it is not just new buildings or renovated facilities that have hidden costs. If a new position is added to a unit to support a new program, more is involved than just salary and benefits. Is there available office space? Is new equipment needed? Is there appropriate support staff? Is reconfiguration of space needed? The answers to these questions will determine the hidden costs of the new program and must be considered in making the final budget decision to support or not support implementing the new program.

Failing to Plan for the End

Budget managers dealing with grant funds often encounter this pitfall. What will happen when the grant is finished? How will the programs or services funded by the grant be funded moving forward? If they are not funded, what are the implications for the institution? Will personnel associated with the grant be terminated? Will they be reassigned? What happens to the equipment?

When a grant is awarded euphoria is high, and it is difficult to get persons involved with the grant to engage in developing alternate scenarios for the end of the funding period. Wishful thinking that the grant will be renewed often is misplaced, and a sensible plan to deal with the closing of the grant needs to be developed at the beginning of the grant period. To do otherwise means expectations of faculty and staff associated with the grant for continued employment would rise, and those served by the program are likely to have expectations that will not be met. Planning for the end should begin at the start.

Failure to Identify Multiyear Consequences

Both people and programs change, and the wise budget manager views those changes through the lens of multiple year fiscal consequences. What is likely to happen, and what will the fiscal consequences be if that scenario plays out? In fact, alternative scenarios that provide sufficient information should be developed for any new program initiative so that decision makers can make an informed decision of whether the gamble of approving the allocation is worth it. The term *gamble* is used deliberately because every new program, new hire, and new piece of equipment is a gamble for the institution. Will the new faculty member develop sufficient research grants and a national reputation in order to justify the funding research laboratory and the requested research assistantships and post docs? Will the new piece of equipment really save staff time and reduce the number of support staff needed in the department? Providing as much information as possible to decision makers helps them make the best decisions that can be made. Part of the information that they need includes the implications for more than the current budget year.

Failing to Understand Implications for Others

There are both intended and unintended consequences for any decision. A responsibility of the unit budget manager is to minimize the unintended consequences of any decision for the entire institution. To illustrate, just because a unit has sufficient funds in the budget does not mean that those funds can be spent without regard to institutional rules, regulations, and salary guidelines. Offering a position to a staff member at a compensation rate that falls outside the institutional guidelines can cause problems for other managers dealing with persons in similar positions. Using funds to purchase equipment such as espresso machines or PDAs for everyone in the unit is likely to cause tension with other parts of the institution. Providing greater travel support than others can access causes ill will. Even if funds are available, expenditures should be in line with institutional guidelines and practices; if unusual expenditures are made, the rationale should be clearly explained.

If the budget unit provides support to other offices and agencies across the institution then any decision to save money by stopping a service must be carefully examined for the unintended consequences it could present to others. To illustrate, if the Information Technology Department decides it will no longer provide technical support for a specific but widely used e-mail program and will only provide technical support to the new e-mail system and program being installed there will be consequences. Some of the consequences might include unhappy faculty and staff, additional costs within departments to purchase outside support for the former e-mail program, and investment of time in training all users in the new system. So is the unilateral decision made by the Information Technology Department really a cost savings to the institution? The answer is clearly no. Understanding the implications of any decision for other offices and agencies is an essential fiscal management tool.

Assuming the Good Times Will Continue

Many institutional and unit budget managers were caught off guard when the traditional sources of funding for higher education dramatically eroded in 2008. Making the assumption that budgets will constantly increase and that inflationary allocations will also be provided is a major error in budgeting and financial management. The astute budget manager should develop alternate plans to respond to a downturn in funding for the department if that should occur.

One of the ways to plan for more fiscally stringent times is to build some flexibility into the current unit operating budget. For example, building an equipment replacement line into the annual operating budget allows the budget manager to replace equipment on a regular and scheduled basis. In addition, it provides a cushion for reallocation in budget years when allocations are not as robust and redistribution between line items is needed. Building such flexibility into the budget is not an easy task because funding for such line items must be carved out of other important priorities in the budget. It will, however, permit a budget manager to have some time to work with colleagues to determine a long-term response to a fiscal crisis. Being forewarned permits the budget manager to be forearmed.

Exhibit 6.1.   Avoiding Pitfalls in Budget Management

Revenue

- Is it accurate or overestimated?
- What assumptions underlie the revenue figures?
- Has the assumption been made that the good times will continue?

Chronic Issues

- Does the submitted budget address long-term and chronic issues?
- Have you established reserve funds for equipment, repair and renovation, or contingencies?
- Is there another office or agency that can help you address a chronic problem?

Beyond the Fiscal Year

- Is there a time-limited grant or contract, and if so what plans are in place for the end of the contract?
- What are the multiyear consequences of the budget decisions made by the unit? Are they defensible?
- What are the hidden costs for each program or project, and are they accounted for in the budget plan?

Beyond the Unit

- What are the implications of the budget decisions beyond the unit budget?
- Have you consulted with those affected?

Advice to New Budget Managers

What insights or advice might be most helpful to new or less experienced budget managers within a department or program? The following suggestions for *success* are compiled from colleagues across the country. These ten suggestions hold true if you are a vice president presenting a budget for an entire division or a director of a small program unit presenting your budget request to your dean or vice president.

Ask Questions

If you are uncertain about something, ask questions. You can save a great deal of time and energy if you seek clarification early in the process rather than later. Do not let your ego get in the way of getting helpful information regarding issues and problems. Bluffing does not work in fiscal management, and be careful not to be bluffed by others.

Be Prepared

Being prepared means doing your homework. You should have sufficient data and backup material at hand so that you can answer questions about expenditures and revenue. You may never be asked for such materials, but you will feel more confident if you have it and can refer to solid data and information when answering questions.

Be Honest

This is a powerful piece of advice and is very important. Being honest is necessary and involves your personal credibility as a budget manager. To be effective a budget manager must be honest and straightforward with others throughout the organization. If a mistake has been made do not try to cover it up but seek good advice on how to deal with the problem and how to avoid such errors in the future.

Being honest also means that you need to provide straightforward feedback to your colleagues within the department when they submit unrealistic budget requests or fail to do the required work that results in a strong budget proposal. Stringing people along without honesty and forthright feedback leaves people feeling frustrated and confused. Just because money is involved does not mean that ethical behavior should not prevail.

Discover What Decision Makers Need

What do the individuals who make budget decisions need to know? What do they care about? What information will have the most meaning for each of the decision makers? Some people want to know comparative data with other, similar institutions. Others are interested in how the unit can contribute to the cost of the request from existing resources (as the old adage says, will you "put your money where your mouth is?"). Still others will want to know how many people will be served. Some decision makers will want to know evaluative data about unit performance. Other individuals will want to see hard data supporting the need for the proposal. Each person involved in the fiscal decision-making process will have different priorities and different needs for information. The key to becoming a successful budget manager is to identify what information decision makers need to make informed choices about the allocation of resources and give it to them. This is not a case where one size fits all.

Don't Play Games

This advice is for both decision makers in budgeting and those making proposals for funding. Nothing is more frustrating than having someone play games in the budget process. It expends time and energy and, when recognized, creates huge credibility problems. The following are among the common forms of budgetary game playing:

- *Game One.* Inflate the budget request, knowing full well that it is unrealistic but hoping that the actual amount of money needed to fund the program will be allocated to the unit.

- *Game Two.* Withhold information from decision maker about either pending revenue or the actual costs associated with the proposal. This approach is foolish at best because the truth will come out through the simple process of doing business.

- *Game Three.* Present only the worst possible scenario when requesting budget support. The reality is usually that the worse possible case will not happen, and budget managers who employ this strategy too often will lose credibility.

- *Game Four.* Sometimes budget managers try to "hide" money in other inflated line items within the unit or in reserve accounts. Such approaches are usually quickly uncovered and raise significant issues of honesty for the budget unit and the integrity of the budget manager.

- *Game Five.* Try to politicize the budget process by involving one or more constituency groups in the process. Students are often used in this approach by asking them to "lobby" the administration for a favorite program. Rarely are good budget decisions made when they are subject to the whims of the student newspaper editorial page.

Identify the Stakeholders and the Decision Makers

The stakeholders of a unit usually are people very different from the decision makers regarding budget matters. Understand the composition of each group and determine what influence they may have on your organization and your budget. A second set of issues involves what information you should share with stakeholder groups. Be very cautious and seek to understand both the implicit and explicit "rules" within the institution.

Learn to Say "I Don't Know"

If you do not know the answer to a question, do not be afraid to say so, but promise you will try to get the answer and get back to the person asking the question by a certain date. It is refreshing for decision makers to work with people who honestly admit when they do not know an answer to a question, and such admissions increase your credibility with others. To be an effective fiscal manager you often need to leave your ego at home.

Pay Attention to Details

Sound fiscal management requires that the unit budget manager pay attention to details. Postings in accounts should be checked for accuracy. Computations should be cross-checked for errors. An effective budget manager cannot just rely on others to provide details on a periodic basis. The unit budget manager must personally review accounts, question expenditures, and focus on long-range projections in a minute sense, as well as deal with the "big picture." Verifying details makes a difference both in credibility and effectiveness.

Make Few Initial Assumptions

Invest time in testing all assumptions in proposals and in the current budget. Sometimes the current budget is accepted as a "given" by a budget manager, and that may not be the case. The assumptions built into the base budget of the unit should be tested for accuracy on a periodic basis for costs and needs that have changed over time. Testing those assumptions provides opportunities for reallocation of resources within the unit. Careful analysis of budget performance of the unit over the last three years can help determine whether the underlying assumptions of the budget are accurate and reflect the current needs of the unit.

Also, any assumptions made in budget proposals should be clearly and explicitly stated as part of the proposal. If the proposed budget is based on a certain participation rate, the rate must be stated. If the proposal is time-limited, that assumption should be made very clear. Remember, however, that when the question is asked whether additional resources will be needed in the future, do not promise more than can be delivered and learn to never say "never," because circumstances and needs change.

Seek Legal Advice When Needed

Contracts for goods and services and personnel issues can consume a great deal of time and energy of a unit budget manager. Consultation should be held with legal counsel prior to signing any contract for goods and services that obligates the institution. If in-house counsel is available, contract review is fairly routine. If outside counsel is used, contract review can become expensive. One strategy is to hold an institutionwide seminar on contracts that provides all budget managers with general basic information about contracts. In addition, institutional policies should limit the dollar amount of a contract that can be signed only by a unit budget manager.

Personnel issues are extraordinarily complex and may be complicated by statutory requirements, current case law, union contract, or other regulations. If you are dealing with a problem employee, seek assistance from the human resources office or legal counsel prior to taking any action.

Effectiveness as a budget manager is as much related to how you approach your work as how you do it. The next section highlights attitudinal issues that can get in the way of effective performance in the role of budget manager.

The Attitude Factor

As indicated earlier, the unit budget manager must be prepared to answer questions and provide data to decision makers. Approaching that process as a confrontational process is a mistake.

When questioned about the reasons for a request or why a certain budget decision was made, defenses sometimes go up and the budget manager gets ready to do battle. Questions by the budget office do not necessarily mean that your judgment is being challenged but may mean that the budget office is seeking information and clarification. Assuming you are under attack immediately places you in a defensive position in any subsequent negotiation and creates unnecessary problems for the unit.

Fiscal management is an important part of the responsibility of most administrators. Taking the position that such activities are beneath you is an invitation to trouble. Disdain for involvement is not an option for the effective budget manager. Investing the time in understanding routine processes and procedures is very smart. Not only will such involvement increase the personal effectiveness of the administrator but also it will create opportunities for the manager to become a better mentor and supervisor.

Expressing unrealistic expectations for other units and people will create an impression of disorganization and confusion within the unit. Every budget manager, at some time, needs to ask for an exception to a rule to meet an emergency situation. But when requests for exceptions become the rule you are in trouble. For example, let's say this morning you realized that in order to pay a pending bill, you need to transfer money from one account into another. The institution has a five day rule for transfers that requires five full days for a transfer to clear. The problem just came to light this morning, and a request for an exception was made. As an exception, staff in the budget and controller's office work with you to clear the transfer and make the payment on time. If, however, such last minute requests are routine from a unit people are less likely to extend themselves to solve the problem. Unrealistic expectations for service and exceptions arise from a sense of entitlement about how important the unit is to the institution. Keeping a sense of perspective is extremely important.

A wise budget manager also recognizes that there are many times when they will be wrong and that their projections, assessments, and plans will not turn out exactly as they were projected. Good budget managers provide their best thinking, but they cannot predict the future. Awareness of your own limitations and those of the system is an important part of being effective in the budget management role.

Finally a unit budget manager is not a lone actor. An effective budget manager works in partnership with others across the institution and within the unit to identify and solve problems.

References

Argyris, C., and Schön, E. *Organizational Learning: A Theory of Action Perspective*. Reading: Addison-Wesley, 1978.

Baldridge, J.V. *Power and Conflict Within the University*. New York: Wiley, 1971.

Barr, M. J. "Internal and External Forces Influencing Programming." In M. J. Barr, L. A. Keating, and Associates (eds.), *Developing Effective Student Services Programs*. San Francisco: Jossey-Bass, 1985.

Barr, M. J., and Golseth, A. E. "Managing Change in a Paradoxical Environment." In M. J. Barr, M. L. Upcraft, and Associates, *New Futures for Student Affairs*. San Francisco: Jossey-Bass, 1990.

Bolman, L. G., and Deal, T. E. *Reframing Organizations: Artistry, Organization, Choice, and Leadership* (3rd ed.). San Francisco: Jossey-Bass, 2003.

Schneider, B. (ed.) *Organization Climate and Culture*. San Francisco: Jossey-Bass, 1990.

Reflection Questions

1. What is the best way to find out the history of financial decision making in your unit?

2. Can you identify the key people, offices, and agencies that the budget manager of your unit should know and work with on a regular basis?

3. What do you think is your biggest challenge in becoming an effective budget manager?

7

Managing Budget Fluctuations

Anyone who serves as a budget manager in higher education for any reasonable length of time is likely to encounter both budget reductions and budget additions in the fiscal environment of their institution. Dealing with budget fluctuations, whether down or up, is never easy, but guidance can be found in the values of the institution. What is the institution trying to accomplish? Who is the institution attempting to serve? How can the institution accomplish those goals within the constraints of budget decisions? Obviously the answers to those questions will be different in each institution, but institutional values are the foundation on which all decisions are made.

This chapter addresses managing budget fluctuations, and it assumes that there is a clear understanding of the values supported by the institution. The chapter begins with a discussion of budget cuts, the reasons that such cuts take place, institutional approaches to budget reductions, and strategies that may assist unit budget managers with the difficult task of reducing costs. Next the chapter turns to the reintroduction of resources into budgets that have been flat or cut. The importance of reflecting on lessons learned during lean economic times, approaches to expanding budgets, the role of priorities in decision making, and suggestions for unit budget managers are all addressed. The chapter closes with concluding thoughts and two case studies that will aid readers in applying information learned throughout the volume.

Reasons for Budget Cuts

The recession of 2008 brought with it many large budget reductions in both independent and public institutions. Although a recession highlights the need for expenditure reduction, budget cuts can occur at any time in higher education and are caused by a number of reasons. Dealing with a budget reduction is very challenging in a college or university because the budget is driven primarily by personnel costs. Cutting personnel is an emotionally laden process that may be complicated as a result of various labor agreements and workforce structures (for example, tenure), and the positive impact on the budget from cutting personnel may not be fully realized for some time whereas the negative impact on the morale and performance of remaining personnel is likely to be immediate.

Budget reductions in institutions of higher education can be caused by a number of factors. The importance of each factor will vary from institution to institution and is directly related to the funding sources used to support a specific institution.

Lower Enrollment

Small private (independent) institutions and those institutions that are state supported are particularly vulnerable to fluctuations in enrollment. For the small private institution a relatively small change in enrollment can make the difference between meeting revenue targets for the budget year and failing to do so. Often in larger private institutions, with endowments, the immediate impact of a drop in enrollment can be absorbed through temporarily changing the amount of money drawn from endowment income during the current fiscal year. Although that strategy cannot be relied on for long it does give institutional administrators time to develop a workable strategy for future financing. In smaller private institutions that have little or no endowment there is a direct and immediate effect of failure to meet enrollment targets, for the institution is dependent on tuition dollars for operating expenses.

For public institutions dependent on formula funding from the state, usually the drop in enrollment is not felt in the current fiscal year but rather is reflected in the next fiscal year allocation from the state. Formula funding for institutions of higher education by state government is in place in most states (see Chapter Three), and an enrollment decline will be factored into the next state appropriation to the institution.

In addition, if an institution has relied on specific academic programs as a major source of revenue, reductions in enrollment in such programs can result in budget reductions. For example, for many years executive MBA programs have provided a lucrative income stream for both business schools and their institutions. To illustrate, at Alpha University, the excess revenue over expenses is split on a fifty-fifty basis between the business school and the university. At its peak that revenue stream was almost one million dollars per year. Enrollment in the program has been gradually declining, and that decline was accelerated by the recession in 2008–2009. Currently the enrollment is approximately 40% of what it was in FY2000. Under these circumstances, the executive MBA program, the business school, and the institution will all experience budget reductions.

Finally, competition for the pool of traditionally aged undergraduate students and nontraditional students can be a factor in enrollment declines. To illustrate, whereas only a few institutions offered executive MBA programs in the early 1990s, those programs are now offered at many colleges and universities. As another example, many community colleges are offering affordable and attractive technological training in two-year programs that are attractive to many students formerly attracted to four-year institutions. Such enrollment shifts from four-year to two-year institutions can influence both the budget of the community college and the four-year institutions in their service areas.

Reductions in Governmental Funding

Governmental funding comes to the institution in many forms, both direct and indirect. Both forms of government funding have been substantially reduced for public institutions whereas private institutions are affected most by reductions in direct student aid.

At the close of fiscal year 2009 the states in total closed with $30 billion dollars in budget shortfalls and faced approximately $200 billion more in budget gaps in the fiscal years 2009 and 2010 (AASCU, 2009). The Center on Budget and Policy Priorities indicated that at least 41 states cut assistance to public colleges and universities in 2009. To cope, some institutions and systems increased tuition in double digit percentages, including California and Florida (Center on Budget and Policy Priorities, 2010).

Student financial aid from both state and federal governments is a prime source of indirect governmental funding; states provide 11% of all grant aid for students and the federal government provides 32% of grant aid (College Board, 2009). Several states made deep cuts in need-based financial aid programs and others held the level of their aid funding constant (Center on Budget and Policy Priorities, 2010). When grant aid is not increased to meet rising educational costs or is reduced at either the state or federal level, the burden of financial aid to students shifts to institutions of higher education and causes great institutional budget stress or enrollment reductions.

It is important to note that colleges and universities are the single largest source of grant aid to students (College Board, 2009). As a result of the recession that began in 2008, institutions were confronted by direct economic pressure and by indirect pressure that resulted from economic constraints on donors.

Direct sources of governmental aid to American higher education are many and have a huge influence on the fiscal health of any institution. Comprehensive institutions, both public and private, rely primarily on governmental funding for research activities. When budget reductions occur at both the federal and state levels the amount of money available to be allocated to institutional research activities is also reduced. Reductions in research funding also occur for reasons other than funding gaps. Sometimes changes occur because governmental priorities change for research, particularly in the area of health and technology. Funds that used to be available to support one kind of research are subsequently diverted to other priorities because of changing societal expectations or pure politics.

Capital projects are also often postponed, cancelled, or drastically reduced when fiscal circumstances of the state or federal government are more constrained. New construction or major remodeling projects usually are easily identified cost centers that can be quickly stopped or never started if funding gaps occur. Also loss of political influence on the part of the institution can cause a reduction in governmental funding. If the institution has had a powerful legislative advocate at either the federal or state level who leaves office, then the funding circumstances of the institution are also likely to change.

Lack of Success in Fundraising

As noted earlier three types of fundraising are important to American higher education: annual fund giving, focused giving for a particular project or program, and large, comprehensive, multiyear campaigns. All can be influenced by the economic conditions in the greater society. Private institutions rely, in part, on annual fund giving to undergird the operating budget of the institution. If economic times change the annual fund is often the first fiscal entity to feel a reduction in support. When the annual fund does not meet its targeted goal, it is likely that there will be reductions in the operating budget both in the current fiscal year and in the next fiscal year as the target will be reduced.

Focused giving for a specific program or building is also influenced by broader economic conditions. If a program is relying on the support of one donor or a group of donors and their sources of income are affected by an economic downturn, their ability to support the program will be diminished. Large, comprehensive, multiyear campaigns can also be influenced both by general economic conditions and by the interests of major donors. Fundraising is not an independent activity but rather one that is intertwined with the greater economic conditions of society.

Unusual or Costly Events

Natural disasters such as hurricanes, floods, earthquakes, mud slides, tornadoes, and other natural disasters can wreak havoc on any institutional budget and result in budget reductions for the foreseeable future. Witness the challenges faced by all of the institutions of higher education in New Orleans and the rest of the Gulf Coast as a result of Hurricane Katrina or the institutions affected by the earthquake in Riverside, California, for example. Even if the umbrella coverage insurance of the institution is available, when a major natural disaster hits losses are often in the millions of dollars. Institutional recovery from a natural disaster is a time-consuming process and has both an immediate and long-term budgetary impact.

Other unusual events can include faulty construction resulting in injuries, fires, laboratory accidents, and other liability claims related to health and safety. If such claims are successful in the courts, legal judgments against the college or university can have a severe budget impact. Even if insurance is present, the initial dollar loss is usually a direct charge to the budget of the institution.

In addition, if there is a large increase in electrical rates and supply due to deregulation or if there is a drop in oil production in OPEC nations, costs for utilities can rise quickly and unexpectedly with great budget consequences. In addition, unexpected increases in health care premiums, postal rates, and insurance costs can also affect budgets negatively. All of these possibilities and many more can have a major influence on the financial health of the institution and can result in budget cuts, particularly if the institution operates with very little room for error in projected budget cost.

Cutting Out the Fat

Some institutions periodically cut budgets by some factor (1 or 2%) on the premise that extra dollars not really needed for operations have crept into the budgeting processes and procedures or as a result of stagnation in other revenue sources. As described in Chapter Three, the amount of money recaptured through such institutionwide budget adjustments are then held at a central institutional level. This pool of recaptured dollars is then used for new and innovative educational ventures or held as a reserve to support future reductions in other funding sources.

Every college or university will probably encounter a reduction in institutional budgets at some time. The wise budget manager should understand why budget reductions are occurring and what strategies are available to the institution as budget reductions are implemented.

Institutional Approaches to Budget Reductions

The institution has several alternatives available when implementing a budget reduction. This section describes issues influencing an institution's choice of approach and discusses various strategies commonly employed by institutions in considering and implementing budget reductions.

Time, Information, and Risk Tolerance

Three issues will influence the institution's approach to budget cuts. They are time, information, and risk tolerance by the institution and the institutional governing board.

The first issue to be addressed is, how much time is available to institute cost savings measures and budget cuts? That is a critical question, for if the reduction must be made in the current fiscal year then the strategies used will be entirely different than if the institution has two or three years to confront a fiscal problem. If a careful plan of cost reductions can be implemented over several years, the results will be much less painful than if the reduction must be made in the current operating budget fiscal year. Goldstein (2005) urges institutions to routinely plan for budget reductions. Although that is a rational approach to the situation, unfortunately, most often budget managers must respond very quickly to an institutional fiscal problem.

The second issue to confront is whether the information available to decision makers is strong and reliable. Underlying assumptions for choosing a specific strategy must be tested so that decision makers are assured that they are making the best possible choice. Questions must be asked about past performance and future income projections, and those questions must be asked in detail. All institutional budget managers should be prepared to provide the data needed to make decisions and should do so in an honest and straightforward manner. For example, if the budget is based on enrollment figures those responsible for predicting the size of the entering class for the next academic year should provide the best data about whether the enrollment target will be met for the coming year. Or if the athletic director is asked to provide his or her best estimate of attendance at home football games for the next year that data should be as accurate as possible. Being overly optimistic does not serve the institution or students well when fiscal issues are at stake.

Finally, decision makers must consider what the tolerance for risk is within the institution and by the governing board. To illustrate, if a long-term planned investment in technology will improve services to students (and perhaps student retention and recruitment), should the institution take the risk of investing in a large technology upgrade when funding is in peril? Is that a good strategic strategy for the institution to take? Toleration for risk will have a great influence on the budget reduction strategy chosen by the institution.

Forms of Budget Reduction

Each institution will choose an institutional budget reduction plan that is unique to its environment. However, there are common forms of budget reduction employed by colleges and universities.

Freeze

A budget freeze is not really a budget reduction, but it may be perceived as one by faculty and staff members in the trenches. Discretionary spending for such items as travel or nonessential purchases is curtailed or stopped when a budget freeze is declared, and major equipment purchases are often postponed. In addition, hiring of new faculty and staff is put on hold and can only occur under special and critical circumstances. A freeze is often used as an interim step while institutional decision makers are attempting to determine the best course of action for the institution. Declaration of a budget freeze is also an effective way to get the attention of faculty and staff regarding the serious nature of the institutional financial problems.

Across-the-Board Cuts

Use of across-the-board cuts is the simplest and most expedient way to manage a budget reduction. Unit budget managers are simply informed that they must cut X% from their budget by a certain date and must specifically report those reductions to the central budgeting authority. The specified percentage may be uniform across the institution, or it may vary by broad administrative category (i.e., academic affairs, financial affairs, or student affairs). The money recaptured from such cuts is used to offset financial problems within the institution or as a tool to avoid deficit spending in the current fiscal year.

The advantage of this strategy is that it provides great flexibility to individual unit administrators and budget managers regarding where cuts can be made. It is also equitable, in one sense, since all budget units within the institution are treated alike. The major flaw of the strategy is that it does not differentiate between budget units that have greater flexibility in their budget allocations and those operating under tight fiscal restraints. The result is that the impact of the across-the-board strategy is that the reductions are felt differentially within the institution and programs critical to the mission of the institution are not protected.

Targeted Reductions

Some institutions chose a targeted reduction strategy that requires cuts in certain line items to achieve savings. Such an approach reduces the flexibility of a unit to respond to a reduction but may provide a more equitable approach to implementing reductions between units. Examples might include targeted reductions in travel, honoraria, equipment replacement, or minor construction projects. Funds originally allocated in these line items are pulled back from the unit budget and held central to meet institutional shortfalls.

The strategy of targeted reductions rests on the premise that some activities are central to institutional purposes whereas others are desirable but less necessary. As part of considering where targeted reductions are to take place, units are asked to justify their expenditures on specific programs and activities such as symposia, retreats, and training. Wise unit budget managers and administrators are prepared for such requests by assuring that they have good evaluative data on the effectiveness of such programs and activities.

Another target reduction strategy is academic or service program elimination. Such decisions should not be entered into lightly and carry with them great potential for disruption and challenges to decisions. A more detailed discussion of this strategy is provided in the section on unit strategies in response to budget cuts (see p. 174).

Restructuring

A more dramatic method for reducing institutional costs involves restructuring the organization of the institution by combining programs and reducing administrative overhead costs. In addition, restructuring can involve changing the way the institution conducts business by instituting new fiscal policies and investing in technology for long-term gains in efficiency and effectiveness.

Organizational restructuring can be a very painful and difficult process. Because people are involved it is fraught with emotion. Examples include collapsing a music school and a visual arts school into one administrative unit renamed the College of Visual and Performing Arts. When such events are considered a number of critical questions must be considered. What programs should be combined? Who should stay and who should go? What is gained and what is lost through any restructuring move? Organizational restructuring can be a very time intensive and painful process, but it can result in substantial savings to the institution.

Establishing and implementing new processes and procedures and examining all aspects of the financial management of the institution is another way to approach restructuring. For example, developing a new banking relationship might improve the return on short-term investments. Restructuring the timing of when purchase orders are processed and paid might result in substantial savings to an institution.

Eliminating Programs

The elimination of programs is never an easy decision but it may be the prudent decision for an institution to make. Priorities change as do interests of students in majors and degrees. If a decision is made to eliminate an academic program careful attention should be paid to the students currently in the program and an assessment made of what is necessary to help them complete their degree aspirations. Such an assessment might include allowing substitute courses or arranging for students to take courses at a nearby institution. Dickeson cautions that it may be necessary to phase in the program elimination until such issues can be satisfactorily resolved (Dickeson, 2010, p. 134).

Whatever form budget reduction takes at their institution, there are a number of strategies that unit administrators and budget managers can adopt that meets the institutional goal while dealing with faculty, staff, and students in the most humane way possible.

Useful Unit Strategies

In a time of budget cuts the jobs of unit members or the programs that they care about can be in jeopardy. When budget reductions occur, morale is a key issue to confront. Some strategies that might be used to meet budget reduction targets in the most humane way are described in this section.

Use The Least Drastic Means First

When personnel issues are involved Dickeson urges institutions to undertake a combination of actions "designed to eliminate, or at least minimize, the impact of outright reductions in force" (2010, p. 134). Such actions can include providing short-term sabbaticals for faculty, leaves with partial pay, furloughs, early retirement packages and leaves without pay, reduction in the number of hours worked, tenure buyouts, and severance packages. None of these actions should be considered without legal advice and careful attention to union contracts and in the case of faculty the AAUP Guidelines for financial exigency.

Share Information

Rumors will abound when budget reductions are announced. The gossip lines will be working overtime both within the department and on the campus. One of the most useful ways to aid colleagues in a time of uncertainty is to provide clear information to them as rapidly as possible. Even if you do not yet fully know what is going on, let staff and faculty members in the unit know that. Trust is reinforced and people, at least, feel that they are being kept informed. When the strategy being employed by the institution is known, share that information with all members of the unit in as clear and concise a manner as possible.

Ask for Suggestions

Once you know the institutional strategy ask for suggestions from your colleagues on how to implement it. There are usually a lot of good ideas within any budget unit, and finding a way to harness those ideas to develop a coherent plan for the unit is invaluable. When asking for suggestions outline the dimensions of the problem for the unit and then specifically ask questions such as the following: In what ways can money be saved or reductions be made within the unit? What suggestions do you have for change? Even if their specific ideas cannot be implemented, your colleagues will have had an opportunity to be heard.

Use Contingency Funds First

Earlier in this volume a suggestion was made to build a contingency fund into the budget for each administrative or program unit. It may be labeled as a contingency, or it may be a line item such as equipment replacement that can be postponed to meet a financial need. Whenever possible a unit should always try to include such flexibility in the operating budget or through reserve funds. Such funds can be the first tapped to respond to a financial emergency at the institutional level.

Ask for Voluntary Cutbacks

If communication has been open and if faculty and staff understand the dimensions of the budget shortfall, it is likely that they will develop some creative solutions that have not yet been considered. Sometimes your colleagues can surprise you with their creativity and willingness to contribute to a solution to a problem facing their unit. There may be individuals, for instance, that would welcome a ten-month appointment as opposed to a twelve-month appointment. There may be others who would like to reduce their status from full time to three-quarters time. Listen to all proposals carefully and honor the sentiments behind them.

In addition, staff colleagues may have suggestions that will not save a great deal of money but are symbolic of their commitment to help confront the issue. Staff agreeing to contribute for office coffee when it had been provided at no charge is one such example. Voluntary reductions only occur as a solution when everyone understands the gravity of the situation.

Make Few Promises

It would be difficult for any unit administrator or budget manager to fully understand the complexity of the financial issues being faced on an institutional level. When required budget cuts occur your managerial options become more limited. It is a time when any manager should make few promises, and those few should be limited to promises that the manager is confident will be honored. Credibility of the budget manager is never more on the line than in difficult economic times. The personal integrity of the budget manager is one of the few "coins of the realm" that a manager possesses under such circumstances. Promise support, provide information, but never say "never" when asked the question of whether any person will lose his or her job.

Cut Back on Nonessentials

Every budget contains nonessential items that are not central to the core of the enterprise. An important step in managing budget reductions at the unit level is to identify and reduce financial commitments to nonessential items. Is the purchase of a specific piece of software essential? Is it necessary for all departmental computers to be replaced in one fiscal year or will replacing only some suffice?

Is new carpeting needed now or can it be postponed for another year? Target those items that would be nice but are not essential.

Consider Outsourcing

Outsourcing or hiring contract services for certain functions may be a means to reduce expenses. Dickeson (2010, pp. 152–153) developed a list of questions that any campus should ask if outsourcing is being considered. They include but are not limited to the following:

1. Is the service to be outsourced part of the strategic vision of the institution?
2. Will outsourcing result in an increase in revenue or a savings in costs?
3. Can the quality of service be maintained or improved?
4. Are actual dollars going to be generated that can then be reallocated?
5. Do the institutional policies (accounting, wage scales, and personnel policies) cause costs to be higher than if the service was contracted?
6. What will the impact be on employee morale?
7. Will the institution still maintain an adequate degree of control if the service is outsourced?
8. What other factors are going to influence the decision to outsource (management, governing board pressures, legal exposure)?

Obviously the decision to outsource should not be entered into lightly. This option should be carefully discussed with decision makers prior to soliciting information from potential vendors.

Look for New Revenue Sources

Consideration might be given to charging for services that were formerly free or adding a service fee to transactions. If such approaches are discussed then a careful analysis needs to be made of whether the additional revenue is enough to offset the costs of collecting the new fee.

Share Resources

With careful planning it may be possible to reduce costs by sharing resources with another budget unit. Equipment is often the easiest commodity to share. Sharing a fax machine, copier, or printer is a real possibility if offices are located in reasonable proximity. In addition, with the right office configuration positions might be shared with reception and initial phone contacts being combined into one position. There are many possibilities. Think creatively with colleagues within the office and the office across the hall.

Be Consistent

Consistency has been an ongoing theme in this volume, and it is essential to success as a budget manager. Managing under difficult circumstances, such as during budget reductions, becomes even more complicated if the manager is not seen as consistent in his or her dealings.

In times of budget reductions (which by definition are times of uncertainty), information will constantly change. As a unit budget manager part of your responsibility is to consistently transmit those changing messages to your colleagues and help them interpret what they might mean. Your fairness and consistency will go a long way in bringing stability to difficult decisions.

Don't Be Afraid to Make Difficult Decisions

When all else fails a unit budget manager must be prepared to make difficult decisions, including termination of employees. Letting someone go is never easy, but it is much more difficult when it is caused by forces and situations outside of the control of the employee or the manager. When faced with such circumstances it is critical that the administrator and budget manager get advice from human resources and sometimes from institutional legal counsel. It is particularly difficult to make a termination decision when a union contract is in place. Failure to follow the provisions of the contract for termination involves potential for lawsuits and work stoppages. Strong legal advice is needed, and the institution needs to have straightforward conversations with union representatives when termination is possible. This is not a set of circumstances where a manager can act alone.

Additional complications occur in termination if the individuals involved are protected by tenure. A careful strategy for dealing with the situation is critical and must involve senior academic administrators, department chairs, and faculty governance groups. Financial exigency is a special case for an institution when reductions involve tenured personnel. The rationale for position elimination needs to be carefully thought out and no other options should be available to the institution (Goldstein, 2005, p. 150). This clearly is a case where a unit budget manager needs permission to move forward and should involve administrative superiors in the process. A fair and impartial process needs to be in place and be executed when such difficult decisions are at stake.

Document the Circumstances, Process, and Outcomes

There may come a time when you or others will need to look back on what happened, review how it was handled, and analyze the budgetary outcomes. Documenting the circumstances necessitating reductions, the process employed in addressing that necessity, and the outcomes of that process can be as simple as a thorough set of notes in an electronic or paper file, but having that information handy could prove invaluable at some point in the future.

Managing Budgetary Opportunities

Although the impact on higher education of the recession that began in 2008 varied by locality and institutional characteristics (Wolverton, 2008), the history of higher education in the United States has been one of sustained growth in enrollments, revenues, and expenses over time. That history tells us that there may come a time when institutions will again find themselves in the position of having some new funding available. Just as good budget managers ought to be prepared to address adverse economic circumstances, they ought to be prepared to respond to economic opportunities when times take a turn for the better.

This section of the chapter suggests a framework for managing and maximizing such opportunities. That framework begins with a series of three questions. What were the lessons from the budget cuts? What approaches ought to be used for reintroducing funds into a budget? What should the priorities be for the new funding? The fourth element of the framework is a set of suggestions for unit managers.

Lessons Learned

It would be a grave disservice to his or her unit for a budget manager to fail to make use of lessons learned during lean budget years to inform budget management decisions when budgetary conditions improve. What has the restriction on budgetary resources revealed about what is essential and what is dispensable to the unit's operation? What new relationships and collaborations born of the necessity to pool resources have proven to be valuable to the unit? How have essential functions and processes been adapted, and do those adaptations have value moving forward? Have new sources of funding been developed that can continue to be drawn upon either for their current purpose or for other purposes?

Approaches

Three of the common approaches for budget cuts described earlier in the chapter suggest models for the reintroduction of funds into a budget. The three suggested models include across-the-board funding, targeted investment, and funding of new programs.

Across-the-Board Funding

Recall that across-the-board reductions in budgets can take the form of a specified reduction in budgets across the entire institution or varying cuts specified by broad organizational area. The same is true for the reintroduction of funds into an institution's budget. Institutions can indicate that all units can increase budgets by X% or they can indicate varying rates for budget increases in academic affairs, financial affairs, and student affairs.

The strengths and limitations of an across-the-board approach to increasing budgets correspond to the strengths and limitations of the approach with regard to cutting budgets. Across-the-board is easy to explain and easy to implement, and it provides flexibility at the unit level. However, it may fail to recognize the critical needs of units that particularly struggled during the preceding budget reductions. It may, like other one-size-fits-all approaches to budget management (incremental budgeting for example), also fail to help assure that resources are directed to institutional priorities.

Targeted Investments

Another approach institutions may pursue in reintroducing funding into budgets is to target investments into strategic priorities. One obvious example is to address salary issues stemming from flat or reduced wages. Similarly, an institution might elect to invest in new positions in priority areas following a period of hiring freezes or staff reductions. Facilities refurbishment or minor equipment replacement that has been on hold is another area that might well be the beneficiary of targeted investments.

Although it does not offer as much flexibility at the unit level as the across-the-board approach, there are advantages to pursuing targeted investments. The approach helps assure that new funds are tightly linked with institutional priorities. Through focusing the use of new dollars in specific areas, targeted investment also helps assure a noticeable impact from the infusion of new funds. Most staff and faculty will experience very little change as the result of a 1% increase in unit budgets across the institution, but the utilization of those same funds to refurbish building entryways or to brighten paint in corridors can have a noticeable impact on day-to-day morale.

Investing in New Programs

A third approach for reintroducing funds into budgets is the creation of new programs. Adding programs can be an expensive proposition, and one axiom of higher education is that it is much easier to start a program than it is to end one. Hence, any decision to add a program ought to undergo thorough and thoughtful consideration. What exactly is the purpose of the new program? How will its success be measured? How would the new program support the institution's mission and priorities? What opportunities exist to identify other sources of support for the new program?

Like targeted investment, the approach of adding new programs can help assure that that the use of new funds is tightly linked to institutional priorities. The creation of new programs, however, can become a politicized process. Some staff and faculty in programs that have had budgets held in check or that have experienced budget cuts may be frustrated to see new programs funded before their interests are addressed.

Priorities

Judgments about priorities are implicit in any decision regarding the reintroduction of resources into the budget. The budgeting process, however, is better served when those judgments are explicit rather than implicit. The list of potential priorities will vary by institution and circumstance. Several common priorities have already been identified in this section: simplicity of process; institutional mission and priorities, morale, and political considerations.

Suggestions

A number of the suggestions offered to unit budget managers earlier in this chapter for dealing with budget cuts may be valuable to those same managers when taking advantage of the availability of new resources. These include the following:

- Sharing information
- Asking for suggestions
- Making few promises
- Being consistent
- Being unafraid to make difficult choices
- Documenting the circumstances, process, and outcomes

How can distributing new resources present difficult choices? It is sometimes easier to explain why nothing is budgeted when it is well known that nothing is available than it is to explain why nothing is budgeted when it is well known that something is available.

Budget managers should also avoid the temptation to simply restore or reinforce what was in place before the budgetary challenges were presented. As noted earlier, attention should be given to lessons learned as a result of recent experiences. The environment in which the institution operates may also have changed. Enrollments may have been affected with regard to number, characteristics of the student body, or both. The local economy may have shifted in ways that require graduates with different skill sets. Public perceptions regarding accountability, quality, or value in higher education may have changed in ways that necessitate or prohibit certain programs or services. Although it was developed for the process of restoring or rebuilding a campus community after a crisis, the advice offered by Jablonski, McClellan, Zdziarski, Ambler, Barnett-Terry, and others (2008) holds true for budget managers in this situation: Build the new normal.

Conclusion

How to do more with less seems to be the question preoccupying budget managers in higher education in the United States and around the world today. However, as Cavanaugh (2009, p. 1.1) observes, "an institution can only 'do more with less' up to the point where 'less' leaves one with 'nothing.'. . . The 'do more with less' mantra works as long as it is possible to make easy cuts. Beyond that, 'doing more with less' either becomes 'doing without' or 'doing fundamentally differently.' That tipping point provides the opportunity for leadership."

It is worth noting that one strategy for proactively addressing fluctuations in budgets is to avoid feast-or-famine behavior. It is not enough to simply selectively add fat to the budget at times of relative abundance and then cut the fat (and often more) at times of scarcity. Budget managers should consistently and critically review budgets and performance with an eye to reconciling them. "What are we doing with what we have, and how well are we doing it?" ought to be the guiding questions of ongoing budget management.

This chapter has offered information for budget managers to help them fulfill their role as leaders in challenging times. However, it has also offered information regarding leading at times of transition between scarce resources and more abundant resources because it is critically important that budget managers be as adept at doing more with more as they are with doing more with less.

Case Studies

The following case studies offer an opportunity to make use of information in this chapter, as well as previous chapters, to address budgetary challenges that might face a higher education institution. Having read through all the chapters, it might also be interesting to return to Chapter One and review the case study on Alpha University at a time of surplus.

Case Study: Omega College

Omega College is a private liberal arts college located in a small town in the Midwest. The closest large city is about fifty miles away. There is a community college in the next town about twenty miles away. Most faculty and staff live in the town or in small towns nearby.

Originally a Protestant-affiliated institution, Omega is now a completely independent institution and receives no funding from the church. It was founded in the late 1800s to meet a pressing need for teachers in the state. Until recently enrollment at Omega has been relatively stable, with average enrollment of 850 full-time undergraduates, some limited programs for part-time students, and a very limited master's degree program in education focusing on certification issues in the state. Undergraduates come to Omega from nearby states, although there is a smattering of students from other areas of the country. There is a very small international student enrollment and most international students study at Omega for a semester and then return home.

Omega has a robust information site on U-Can (the University and College Accountability Network). The cost of tuition is $25,000 for the academic year and room and board is an additional $7800 for two semesters. About 70% of the full-time students who attend Omega receive some type of financial aid (state, federal, and/or institutional).

In each of the last four years the freshman enrollment has missed the target by about twenty students. To offset that enrollment drop, the admissions staff developed an outreach program to the nearby community college to encourage transfer students, but most of the community college transfer students go to the regional campus of the state university to complete their bachelor's degree. There is a nearby military base, but students rarely come to Omega from that source. The average enrollment over the last four years has dropped to 800 full-time students. This is of concern for many reasons, not the least of which is the financial health of the institution.

Omega has a very limited endowment (most of which is earmarked for student financial aid, some academic departmental support, and three endowed professorships) and thus is very dependent on undergraduate tuition to meet the day-to-day operating expenses of the institution. Graduate tuition for the part-time teacher certification program is a financial plus for the institution.

An annual fund program is essential to the fiscal health of the institution and relies on the generosity of board members, alumni, and friends of the institution to help fund the annual operating budget. The decline in enrollment has caused the institution to reduce nonessential budget expenditures, and faculty and staff have not received a raise for the past two years. Obviously, Omega College is just holding on and a new approach to financing the ongoing expenses of the institution is needed.

The institutional administration and faculty and the governing board are currently focused on development of a strategic plan for the institution that deals with both the financial and enrollment questions. The strategic planning committee is charged with the following responsibilities:

1. The development of a five-year financial plan for the institution.

2. The development of an academic plan that increases the options and opportunities for students to come to Omega College at the undergraduate and graduate levels.

3. The development of an aggressive institutional advancement plan. As the committee does its work the college administration must work to stabilize enrollment and keep the doors of the institution open.

As a member of the administration:

1. What other actions might you recommend that the institution consider for the short term?

2. What additional sources of revenue could you identify that might be available to Omega College?

3. What data would you need to gather to determine whether the options being considered are viable and cost effective?

Case Study: Challenging Times at Alpha University

Alpha University is a midsized public institution in a state where institutions receive some support from the state (which varies from year to year), has a modest endowment, is dependent on mandatory fees to provide many student services (recreation, intercollegiate athletics, health service), is able to retain the tuition revenue at the local level that is generated through enrollment, and has a modest research program that has been remarkably successful.

As a result of a 2% cut in support per student from state appropriations, increases in the costs of employee benefits and utilities, and an agreement to settle a legal claim, Alpha University faces a projected deficit of $7 million for the next fiscal year.

The projected budget includes the following specific budget issues that must be resolved:

- Health insurance costs have skyrocketed, resulting in a premium increase for the next fiscal year. If fully funded the estimated cost for the institutional share would be $650,000.

- After a Title IX complaint an agreed upon plan with the Office of Civil Rights involves an increase in support for women's intercollegiate athletics (estimated cost: $450,000 in the first year, $300,000 a year thereafter).

- Assuming no changes in use, the cost of natural gas is rising, resulting in an institutional budget increase for the next fiscal year (estimated cost: $400,000).

- The university budget committee has received budget increase requests totaling more than $14 million for the next fiscal year.

- Requests have been received for the next academic year for additional faculty positions to cover increased demand for required core courses. There has been an increase in student complaints regarding their inability to get into needed core courses in a timely manner and inquiries have come from parents and legislators. If fully funded the estimated cost would be $750,000.

- An unanticipated increase in postal rates has resulted in an increase in the total institutional base budget for postage (estimated cost: $27,000).

- The vice president for information technology indicates that the first phase of a three-year upgrade of the network and supporting software must begin in the next fiscal year. The estimated cost would be $1.5 million.

- The counseling center has a long waiting list and is requesting two additional positions for the regular academic year and one for the entire fiscal year. If fully funded, the estimated cost including benefits and increased malpractice premiums would be $270,000.

- The governing board would like to attract more National Merit Scholars and has strongly suggested that the institution present a budget with a substantial increase in the institutional base budget for that purpose. The estimated cost if fully funded would be $500,000 per year.

Additional requests have been received as follows:

1. The physical plant would like to implement a five-year program of installation of programmable thermostats in all academic buildings to reduce heating costs at night and the weekend (estimate cost: $250,000; would pay for itself in five years).

2. New lab equipment in the department of chemistry (estimated cost: $200,000).

3. New furniture for the student center lounge that has not been replaced since the building opened 15 years ago (estimated cost: $550,000).

4. Resurfacing of parking lots in the north campus (estimated cost: $250,000).

5. The establishment of a center to improve writing for students at both the undergraduate and graduate levels (estimated cost for reconstruction of space and hiring of staff: $1.7 million).

6. Addition of a new master's degree program in integrated management (estimated cost: $1 million, estimated to pay for itself in six years).

7. Reconstruction of interview space in the Career Planning and Placement area (estimated cost: $400,000).

8. Establishment of a freshman seminar program for all entering first-year students regardless of major (estimated cost: $825,000).

9. Development of a strong alumni network for career planning (estimated cost: $100,000).

10. Adding two intramural playing fields with lights on undeveloped land (estimated cost: $1.2 million).

11. Development of a child care support program for faculty, staff, and students (estimated cost: $750,000).

The task of the budget committee is to make recommendations to the president regarding what budget cuts and what new investments should be made for the next year. As members of the committee you must decide what recommendations to make to the president. As part of that recommendation you must answer the following questions:

1. What criteria will be used in setting priorities?

2. What political or other internal campus dynamics may influence the decisions?

3. What mandates exist that must be funded?

4. What adjustments would you make in the requests?

5. How would you prioritize the revised requests?

6. What strategies would you employ to find the funds to meet Alpha University's needs and aspirations?

References

American Association of State Colleges and Universities. "Top 10 State Policy Issues for Higher Education in 2009." *Policy Matters*, January 2009. Accessed on July 27, 2010, at http://www.aascu.org/media/pm/pdf/pmjan09.pdf.

Cavanaugh, J. C. "Leadership in the Great Recession." In M. Fennell and S. D. Miller (Eds.), *Presidential Perspectives*. Philadelphia: Aramark, 2009.

Center on Budget and Policy Priorities. *An Update on State Budget Cuts*. Accessed on July 27, 2010, at http://www.cbpp.org/cms/?fa=view&id=1214.

College Board. "Economic Challenges Lead to Lower Non-tuition Revenues and Higher Prices at Colleges And Universities." Accessed on December 26, 2009, at http://www.collegeboard.com/press/releases/208962.html.

Dickeson, R. *Prioritizing Academic Programs and Services* (2nd ed.). San Francisco: Jossey-Bass, 2010.

Goldstein, L. *College and University Budgeting*. Washington, D.C.: National Association of College and University Business Officers, 2005.

Jablonski, M., McClellan, G. S., Zdziarski, E., Ambler, D., Barnett-Terry, R., Cook, L., Dunkle, J. H., Gatti, R., Griego, E., and Kindle, J. (2008). *In Search of Safer Communities: Emerging Practices for Student Affairs in Addressing Campus Violence*. Washington, D.C.: NASPA.

Wolverton, B. "How Might a Recession Impact Higher Education?" *Chronicle of Higher Education*, March 28, 2008. Accessed on December 26, 2009, at http://chronicle.com/article/How-Might-a-Recession-Impact/6367.

Glossary of Terms

Accrual—method of accounting that recognizes revenues at the time they are earned and expenses at the time they are committed regardless of whether or not cash has actually been received or disbursed

All-funds budgets—budgeting system that takes into account all forms of revenue and expense thereby offering a holistic view of the institutional budget

Appropriated funds—funds provided by states to support either operating expenses or capital projects

Auxiliary—unit that is expected to stand on its own with regard to budget, receiving very little financial support from the central institution budget

Bonds—financial instrument that an institution can issue for sale (subject to policy and statutory limitations regarding taking on debt and to the institution's credit worthiness), allowing the institution to raise funds with the promise of repayment of the principal plus interest at a specified point in the future

Budget cycle—15–18 month annual process of creating, managing, and closing a budget

Budget manager—individual who as part of his or her responsibilities is charged with the primary role in creating, managing, and closing a unit budget

Budget statement—report reflecting base budget, financial activity for the specified period (for example, a given month), and year-to-date activity

Capital budget—budget established for the purpose of the financial management of a specified capital project such as the construction or major renovation of a building

Change order—change to the specifications for a capital project coming after the final drawings and proposals are approved; typically results in an additional charge to the capital budget for the project

Consumer Price Index (CPI)—standard used to measure the growth or decline of the cost of goods and services in the general economy

Cost accounting—management accounting tool that identifies actual costs of programs, operations, or processes to permit better management practices

Cost center—service or program unit that is not expected to be self-sustaining with regard to budget

Debt service—scheduled payments made to fulfill debt obligations, including both principal and interest

Deferred maintenance—annualized value of renovation of replacement of major facility infrastructure such as roofs, windows, or plumbing over the scheduled life of that particular infrastructure system

Designated funds—portion of expenses that have been earmarked for a specific purpose

Direct costs—expenses that can be directly associated with a given activity, program, or service

Endowment income—proceeds resulting from the investment of endowment funds

Fee-for-service—direct charge to the user of an activity, program, or service

Financial exigency—state of extreme financial duress sufficient that it threatens the survival of the institution as a whole; requires a formal declaration by the institution, which then allows it to terminate faculty employment for financial cause regardless of tenure status

Fiscal year—specified 12-month period constituting the budget year

Formula budgeting—budgeting system that relies on the use of specified criteria in allocating resources

Functional classification—method of organizing and expressing revenue and expenses in a budget according to purpose

Fungible—quality of funds that can be substituted or exchanged from one purpose to another (e.g., office supplies funds that may be used to supplement funds for purchasing software)

Higher Education Cost Adjustment (HECA)—replacement index for the HEPI, which was introduced by the State Higher Education Executive Officers to correct past deficiencies (HEPI salary data were self-referential) and to offer a more valid tool for measuring higher education inflation; composed of 75% salary data, generated by the federal Employment Cost Index, and 25% from the federal Gross Domestic Price Deflator

Higher Education Price Index (HEPI)—standard used to measure the growth or decline of the cost of goods and services in higher education; an approximation of what colleges, as opposed to families, buy, which includes an analysis of faculty salaries based on AAUP data and a representation of several price indexes for other commodities that institutions purchase

Incremental budgeting—budgeting system that establishes across-the-board percentage changes in expenditures based on assumptions regarding revenues for the coming year

Indirect costs—costs for goods and services that are not directly attributable to particular units but rather benefit all units in an organization

Initiative-based budgeting—budgeting system that requires units to return a portion of their budgets for the purposes of funding new initiatives

Line-item—traditional budget format that identifies objects-of-expenditure (salaries, benefits, travel, etc.) rather than their intended programmatic use

Mandatory fees—fees charged to all students to support institutional services such as student activities or technology services

Natural classification—method of organizing and expressing revenue and expenses in a budget according to type

Operating budget—core budget of an institution reflecting all revenue expenses

Overhead—portion of expenses for indirect costs assigned to particular units

Performance-based budgeting—budgeting system that allocates resources premised on attainment of performance measures

Planning, programming, and budget systems (PPBS)—budgeting system premised on tightly integrating strategic planning, budgeting, and assessment

Reserve funds—funds accumulated and held to address unanticipated challenges and opportunities or to address deferred maintenance or renovation needs

Responsibility center budgeting—budgeting system that sees units as either revenue or cost centers and locates responsibility for unit budget performance at the local level

Restricted funds—funds allocated, collected, or donated for a specific purpose

Retrenchment—significant cutting of activities, programs, or services as a result of financial constraints

Revenue center—budget unit able to generate revenue through its operations

Rolling average—average level of expense or revenue over a specified period of time

Special funds budget—budget established for designated programs or services

Unrestricted funds—funds available for any generally permissible institutional purpose

Zero-based budgeting—budget system in which each item in the budget must be justified at the time the budget is developed

Index